First World War
and Army of Occupation
War Diary
France, Belgium and Germany

56 DIVISION
Divisional Troops
282 and 283 Brigade Royal Field Artillery,
Divisional Trench Mortar Batteries
and Divisional Ammunition Column
1 October 1915 - 28 May 1919

WO95/2941

The Naval & Military Press Ltd
www.nmarchive.com
Published in association with The National Archives

Published by

The Naval & Military Press Ltd

Unit 10 Ridgewood Industrial Park,

Uckfield, East Sussex,

TN22 5QE England

Tel: +44 (0) 1825 749494

www.naval-military-press.com

www.nmarchive.com

This diary has been reprinted in facsimile from the original. Any imperfections are inevitably reproduced and the quality may fall short of modern type and cartographic standards.

© **Crown Copyright**
Images reproduced by permission of The National Archives, London, England, 2015.

Contents

Document type	Place/Title	Date From	Date To
Heading	WO95/2941/1		
Heading	56th Division 282nd (C. Of L) Bde RFA Formerly 1/3 London Bde 1915 Oct-1916 Dec To 1 Army		
Heading	56 Div Troops Attached 36 Div 1/3rd London Bde R.F.A. 1915 Oct-1916 Feb		
Heading	1/3 London Bde R.F.A. Vol V		
Miscellaneous	1/3rd London Brigade R.F.A.	31/08/1915	31/08/1915
Heading	1/3rd Bde (London) R.F.A. Vol I Oct 15-Nov 15		
Heading	War Diary Of 1/3 London Brigade R.F.A. From 1st Oct To 31st Oct		
War Diary	Bordon	01/10/1915	04/10/1915
War Diary	Havres	05/10/1915	05/10/1915
War Diary	Arqoeuves	06/10/1915	20/10/1915
War Diary	Sailly	21/10/1915	30/10/1915
War Diary	Hem	31/10/1915	31/10/1915
War Diary	Bordon	01/10/1915	04/10/1915
War Diary	Southampton	04/10/1915	04/10/1915
War Diary	Havre	05/10/1915	05/10/1915
War Diary	Arqoeuves	06/10/1915	20/10/1915
War Diary	Thievres	21/10/1915	21/10/1915
War Diary	Sailly	22/10/1915	30/10/1915
War Diary	Thievres	31/10/1915	31/10/1915
Miscellaneous	Roll Of Officers Left Behind With Details	02/10/1915	02/10/1915
Heading	War Diary Of 1/3rd London Brigade R.F.A. From 1st Nov 1915 To 30th Nov 1915		
War Diary	Hem	01/11/1915	28/11/1915
War Diary	Mesnil	29/11/1915	30/11/1915
Heading	1/3 London Bde R.F.A. Dec Vol II		
Heading	1/3rd London Bde R.F.A. War Diary Dec		
War Diary	Mesnil	01/12/1915	11/12/1915
War Diary	Thiennes	12/12/1915	19/12/1915
War Diary	Fosse	20/12/1915	31/12/1915
Miscellaneous	Daily Report On Enemy Artillery	23/12/1915	23/12/1915
Miscellaneous	Daily Report On Enemy Artillery	24/12/1915	24/12/1915
Miscellaneous	Daily Report On Enemy Artillery	25/12/1915	25/12/1915
Miscellaneous	Daily Report On Enemy Artillery	26/12/1915	26/12/1915
Miscellaneous	Daily Report On Enemy Artillery	27/12/1915	27/12/1915
Miscellaneous	Daily Report On Enemy Artillery	28/12/1915	28/12/1915
Miscellaneous	Daily Report On Enemy Artillery	29/12/1915	29/12/1915
Miscellaneous	Daily Report On Enemy Artillery	30/12/1915	30/12/1915
Miscellaneous	Daily Report On Enemy Artillery	31/12/1915	31/12/1915
Miscellaneous	Daily Report On Enemy Artillery	22/12/1915	22/12/1915
Miscellaneous	Daily Report On Enemy Artillery	23/12/1915	23/12/1915
Miscellaneous	Daily Report On Enemy Artillery	24/12/1915	24/12/1915
Miscellaneous	Daily Report On Enemy Artillery	25/12/1915	25/12/1915
Miscellaneous	Daily Report On Enemy Artillery	26/12/1915	26/12/1915
Miscellaneous	Daily Report On Enemy Artillery	27/12/1915	27/12/1915
Miscellaneous	Daily Report On Enemy Artillery	28/12/1915	28/12/1915
Miscellaneous	Daily Report On Enemy Artillery	29/12/1915	29/12/1915
Miscellaneous	Daily Report On Enemy Artillery	30/12/1915	30/12/1915

Miscellaneous	Daily Report On Enemy Artillery	31/12/1915	31/12/1915
Heading	47th Division 1-3rd London Brigade RFA Jan-Feb 1916		
Heading	War Diary Of 1/3rd London Brigade R.F.A. From 1st To 31st January 1916		
War Diary	Fosse	01/01/1916	01/01/1916
War Diary	Faucquenhem	02/01/1916	02/01/1916
War Diary	Ames	03/01/1916	08/01/1916
War Diary	Lieres	09/01/1916	23/01/1916
Miscellaneous	4th Divisional Artillery-General Report	29/01/1916	29/01/1916
Miscellaneous	47th Divisional Artillery-General Report		
Heading	1/3 London Bde R.F.A. Feb Vol III		
War Diary	Lieres	24/01/1916	26/01/1916
War Diary	Les Brebis	27/01/1916	18/02/1916
War Diary	Ames	19/02/1916	24/02/1916
War Diary	Headquarters At Caumont	25/02/1916	26/02/1916
War Diary	Francieres	27/02/1916	29/02/1916
Miscellaneous	47th Div Arty	30/01/1916	30/01/1916
Miscellaneous	47th Divisional Artillery-General Report	01/02/1916	01/02/1916
Miscellaneous	47th Divisional Artillery-General Report	02/02/1916	02/02/1916
Miscellaneous	47th Divisional Artillery-General Report	03/02/1916	03/02/1916
Miscellaneous	47th Divisional Artillery-General Report	04/02/1916	04/02/1916
Miscellaneous	47th Divisional Artillery-General Report	05/02/1916	05/02/1916
Miscellaneous	47th Divisional Artillery-General Report	06/02/1916	06/02/1916
Miscellaneous	47th Divisional Artillery-General Report	07/02/1916	07/02/1916
Miscellaneous	47th Divisional Artillery-General Report	08/02/1916	08/02/1916
Miscellaneous	47th Divisional Artillery-General Report	09/02/1916	09/02/1916
Miscellaneous	47th Divisional Artillery-General Report	10/02/1916	10/02/1916
Miscellaneous	47th Divisional Artillery-General Report	11/02/1916	11/02/1916
Miscellaneous	47th Divisional Artillery-General Report	12/02/1916	12/02/1916
Miscellaneous	47th Divisional Artillery-General Report	13/02/1916	13/02/1916
Miscellaneous	47th Divisional Artillery-General Report	14/02/1916	14/02/1916
Miscellaneous	47th Divisional Artillery-General Report	15/02/1916	15/02/1916
Miscellaneous	47th Divisional Artillery-General Report	16/02/1916	16/02/1916
Miscellaneous	47th Divisional Artillery-General Report	17/02/1916	17/02/1916
Miscellaneous	47th Divisional Artillery-General Report	18/02/1916	18/02/1916
War Diary	Francieres	01/03/1916	12/03/1916
War Diary	Autheux	13/03/1916	16/03/1916
War Diary	Bouret Sur Canche	17/03/1916	31/03/1916
War Diary	Bouret	01/04/1916	30/04/1916
War Diary	Bouret-Sur-Canche	01/05/1916	07/05/1916
War Diary	Souastre	08/05/1916	23/06/1916
War Diary	Hebuterne	24/06/1916	03/07/1916
War Diary	Fonquevillers	04/07/1916	13/07/1916
War Diary	Bienvillers	14/07/1916	31/07/1916
Heading	56th Divisional Artillery 282nd Brigade Royal Field Artillery August 1916		
War Diary	Bienvillers	01/08/1916	31/08/1916
Heading	56th Divisional Artillery 282nd Brigade R.F.A. September 1916		
War Diary	Pas	01/09/1916	01/09/1916
War Diary	Le Meillard	02/09/1916	04/09/1916
War Diary	Douars	05/09/1916	30/09/1916
Heading	War Diary November 1916 282nd Brigade R.F.A. Vol 12		
War Diary	Mametz	01/11/1916	01/11/1916

War Diary	Douars	02/11/1916	02/11/1916
War Diary	Molliens	03/11/1916	03/11/1916
War Diary	Amplier	04/11/1916	04/11/1916
War Diary	Bouret	05/11/1916	05/11/1916
War Diary	G.9.b	06/11/1916	29/11/1916
War Diary	Laresset	30/11/1916	30/11/1916
Heading	War Diary 282nd Bde RFA December 1916 Vol 13		
War Diary	Laresset	01/12/1916	04/12/1916
War Diary	Laventie	05/12/1916	31/12/1916
Heading	WO95/2941/2		
Heading	56 Div 283 Bde RFA Formerly 1/4 Lond Bde 1915 Oct-1916 Sep		
Heading	56 Div Troops 1/4th London Bde R.F.A. Oct Nov 1915		
Miscellaneous	1/4th London Howitzer Brigade	31/08/1915	31/08/1915
Miscellaneous	1/4th London Howitzer Brigade	27/09/1915	27/09/1915
Heading	36th Division 1/4th London Bde R.F.A. Vol I Oct 15 Dec 15		
Heading	War Diary Of 1/4 London (How) Bde R.F.A.T. From Oct 1.1915 To Oct 31.1915 Volume I		
War Diary	Bordon	01/10/1915	03/10/1915
War Diary	Havre	04/10/1915	05/10/1915
War Diary	Vaux-En-Amienois	06/10/1915	20/10/1915
War Diary	Mailly	22/10/1915	30/10/1915
War Diary	Bonneville	31/10/1915	31/10/1915
War Diary	Havre	03/10/1915	05/10/1915
War Diary	Vaux	06/10/1915	20/10/1915
War Diary	Forceville	21/10/1915	31/10/1915
Heading	1/4 London Bde R.F.A. Nov Vol II		
Heading	War Diary Of 1/4th London (How) Bde R.F.A.T. From Nov 1 1915 To Nov 30 1915 Volume I		
War Diary	Bonneville	01/11/1915	28/11/1915
War Diary	Les Masures	29/11/1915	30/11/1915
Miscellaneous			
Heading	War Diary Of 1/4 London Howitzer Brigade R.F.A. From December 1st 1915 To Dec 31st 1915 Volume 1		
War Diary	Les Masures	01/12/1915	11/12/1915
War Diary	Pont Remy	12/12/1915	12/12/1915
War Diary	Pecqueur	13/12/1915	18/12/1915
War Diary	Pecqueur-Corbie	19/12/1915	19/12/1915
War Diary	Corbie	20/12/1915	23/12/1915
War Diary	Corbie-Glomenghem	24/12/1915	24/12/1915
War Diary	Glomenghem	25/12/1915	31/12/1915
Heading	Dismounted Cavalry Division Divisional Arty 1-4th London Howitzer Bde R.F.A. Jan-Feb 1916		
Miscellaneous	Dismounted Division	01/02/1916	01/02/1916
War Diary	Glomenghem	01/01/1916	05/01/1916
War Diary	Novelles Les Vermelles	06/01/1916	10/01/1916
War Diary	Vermelles	11/01/1916	12/01/1916
War Diary	Noyelles Les Vermilles	13/01/1916	19/01/1916
War Diary	Vermelles	20/01/1916	31/01/1916
Heading	1/4th London How Bde. R.F.A. War Diary For February 1916		
War Diary	Vermelles	01/02/1916	22/02/1916
War Diary	Ecquedecques	23/02/1916	29/02/1916
Miscellaneous	Cavalry Corps	22/02/1916	22/02/1916

Heading	War Diary 1/4 London Howitzer Brigade R.F.A. 1st March 1916-31st March 1916 Vol V		
War Diary	Berneuil	01/03/1916	12/03/1916
War Diary	Outrebois	13/03/1916	15/03/1916
War Diary	Wamin-Roziere	15/03/1916	31/03/1916
War Diary	Wamin	01/04/1916	30/04/1916
Heading	283rd Brigade R.F.A. Late 1/4 London Bde War Diary For May, 1916		
War Diary	Wamin	01/05/1916	07/05/1916
War Diary	Pas	08/05/1916	21/05/1916
Miscellaneous	Appendix "A" Officer Commanding, 283rd Brigade, R.F.A.	26/05/1916	26/05/1916
War Diary	Pas	22/05/1916	27/05/1916
War Diary	Sailly-Au-Bois	28/05/1916	31/05/1916
War Diary	Sailly	01/06/1916	11/06/1916
War Diary	Pas	12/06/1916	15/06/1916
War Diary	Henu	16/06/1916	30/06/1916
Heading	To 56th Divisional Artillery War Diary Of 283rd Brigade R.F.A. (& Centre Group) For July 1916		
War Diary	Henu	01/07/1916	10/07/1916
War Diary	Chateau De La Haie	11/07/1916	31/07/1916
Heading	56th Divisional Artillery 283rd Brigade Royal Field Artillery August 1916		
War Diary	Chateau La Haie	01/08/1916	31/08/1916
Heading	56th Divisional Artillery (Right Group) 283rd Brigade R.F.A. September 1916		
War Diary	Mezerolles	01/09/1916	01/09/1916
War Diary	Le Meillard	02/09/1916	03/09/1916
War Diary	Cardonette	04/09/1916	04/09/1916
War Diary	Daours	05/09/1916	05/09/1916
War Diary	Near Bray.s.5	06/09/1916	12/09/1916
War Diary	Near Maricourt	13/09/1916	30/09/1916
Heading	WO95/2941/3		
Heading	56th Division Divl Trench Mortar Btys May 1917-Jan 1919		
Map	Map		
Heading	War Diary Trench Mortar Batteries 56th Divisional Artillery May-1917		
War Diary	Achiecourt	01/05/1917	27/05/1917
War Diary	S.2.d.50.15	28/05/1917	31/05/1917
Heading	War Diary 56th Divisional Artillery T.M. Batteries June 1917 Vol 2		
War Diary	Ligny St. Flochel	01/06/1917	14/06/1917
War Diary	S2.d.50.15	01/06/1917	14/06/1917
War Diary	Ligny St Flochel	15/06/1917	30/06/1917
Heading	56th Divnl Artillery Trench Mortar Batteries War Diary July 1917 Vol III		
War Diary	Boiry-Le-Mont	01/07/1917	04/07/1917
War Diary	S2.d.50.15	04/07/1917	05/07/1917
War Diary	Abbeville	06/07/1917	06/07/1917
War Diary	Proven	07/07/1917	08/07/1917
War Diary	International Corner	09/07/1917	11/07/1917
War Diary	A.12.b.2.5	12/07/1917	20/07/1917
War Diary	A.5.d.0.8.	21/07/1917	31/07/1917
Miscellaneous	56th Div Arty. Trench Mortar Batteries	31/07/1917	31/07/1917
War Diary	A.5.d.0.8	01/08/1917	06/08/1917

War Diary	G.23.d.9.1	07/08/1917	31/08/1917
Heading	War Diary 56th Divisional Artillery Trench Mortar Batteries September 1917 Vol 5		
War Diary	Ouderdoom	01/09/1917	03/09/1917
War Diary	Bapaume	04/09/1917	07/09/1917
War Diary	Morchies	08/09/1917	30/09/1917
Miscellaneous	56th Division A.Q.X. 541	10/05/1917	10/05/1917
War Diary	Morchies	01/10/1917	30/11/1917
Miscellaneous	Summary Of Special Operations	20/11/1917	20/11/1917
War Diary	Morchies	01/12/1917	12/12/1917
War Diary	Anzin	13/12/1917	31/12/1917
Heading	War Diary 56th D.A. TM B's January 1918 Vol 9		
War Diary	Anzin	01/01/1918	08/01/1918
War Diary	Cambligneul	09/01/1918	09/02/1918
War Diary	Simcoe Camp (Near Roclincourt)	10/02/1918	27/02/1918
Heading	War Diary 56th Divisional Artillery Trench Mortar Batteries March 1918		
Heading	56th Divisional Artillery Trench Mortar Batteries War Diary March 1918 Vol 11		
War Diary	Simcoe Camp Nr Roclincourt	01/03/1918	30/03/1918
War Diary	Anzin	31/03/1918	31/03/1918
Heading	Appendices 1,2 And 3		
Operation(al) Order(s)	56th Divisional Artillery Trench Mortar Operation Order No. 12	08/03/1918	08/03/1918
Operation(al) Order(s)	56th Divisional Artillery Order No. 23	16/03/1918	16/03/1918
Miscellaneous	Appendix No.3 6" Medium Trench Mortar Report of the Operations of the 28th March 1918.	30/03/1918	30/03/1918
Heading	56th Divisional Artillery 56th Divisional Trench Mortars April 1918		
War Diary	Ecoivres	01/04/1918	09/04/1918
War Diary	Montenescourt	10/04/1918	14/04/1918
War Diary	Simencourt	15/04/1918	27/06/1918
Heading	War Diaries H.Q. 56th Div. Arty 280th Brigade R.F.A. 281st Brigade, R.F.A. 56th D.A.C. X & Y/56 T.M Batteries July 1918		
War Diary	Simencourt	03/07/1918	21/07/1918
War Diary	Aubigny	22/07/1918	30/07/1918
War Diary	Simencourt	31/07/1918	31/07/1918
Heading	56D TM Bty Vol 15		
War Diary	Simencourt	01/08/1918	22/08/1918
War Diary	Wailly	24/08/1918	24/08/1918
War Diary	S.8.b.85.85	27/08/1918	27/08/1918
War Diary	Boisleaux Au Mont	01/09/1918	06/09/1918
War Diary	Arras	07/09/1918	20/09/1918
War Diary	Saudemont	21/09/1918	30/09/1918
Miscellaneous	Appendix "I" Special Operations. 27.9.18.	30/09/1918	30/09/1918
Miscellaneous	Appendix To 56th Divisional Artillery Operation Order No. 66	25/09/1918	25/09/1918
War Diary	Saudemont	01/10/1918	17/10/1918
War Diary	Escadoeuvres	22/10/1918	11/11/1918
War Diary	Onnezies	15/11/1918	31/12/1918
War Diary	Ciply	01/01/1919	31/01/1919
Heading	WO95/2941/4		
Heading	56th Division 56th Divl Ammn Column Feb 1916-May 1919		
Heading	War Diary 56th D.A.C. Late 10th D.A.C Feb Vol 5		

War Diary	Lespesses	17/02/1916	25/02/1916
War Diary	Erondelle	26/02/1916	27/02/1916
War Diary	St Leger	27/02/1916	27/02/1916
Heading	War Diary 56th Div. Ammn Col. R.F.A. Vol VI February 1916 Vol VI		
War Diary	St. Leger	04/03/1916	12/03/1916
War Diary	Hem	15/03/1916	15/03/1916
War Diary	Etre-Wamin	17/03/1916	31/03/1916
Heading	War Diary 56 Div. Am. Col. R.F.A. For April 1916 Vol VII		
War Diary	Etree-Wamin	05/04/1916	05/04/1916
War Diary	In Billets	16/04/1916	29/04/1916
Heading	War Diary 56th Div. Amm. Col R.F.A. Vol 8		
War Diary	Etree Wamin	08/05/1916	08/05/1916
War Diary	Mondicourt	13/05/1916	27/05/1916
Heading	War Diary For Month Of June 1916 56 D.A.C. R.F.A.		
War Diary	Mondicourt	10/06/1916	15/06/1916
War Diary	Henu	21/06/1916	30/06/1916
Heading	War Diary July 1916 56 Div Am. Col. R.F.A. Vol 10		
War Diary	Henu	05/07/1916	25/07/1916
Heading	War Diary 56 D.A.C R.F.A. 1-8-16 31-8-16 Vol XI		
War Diary	Henu	01/08/1916	30/08/1916
War Diary	Mezerolles	31/08/1916	31/08/1916
Heading	56th Divisional Artillery 56th Divisional Ammunition Column R.F.A. September 1916		
War Diary	Genne-Ivergny	01/09/1916	01/09/1916
War Diary	Bois Bergues	03/09/1916	03/09/1916
War Diary	Villers-Bocage	04/09/1916	04/09/1916
War Diary	Daours	06/09/1916	06/09/1916
War Diary	62d.f.25.b.8.2	07/09/1916	10/09/1916
War Diary	F29.b.7.7	12/09/1916	28/09/1916
Heading	War Diary 56 D.A.C. November 1916 Vol 14		
War Diary	F 17.c.6.8	01/11/1916	01/11/1916
War Diary	Daours	02/11/1916	02/11/1916
War Diary	Villers-Bocage	03/11/1916	03/11/1916
War Diary	Orville	04/11/1916	04/11/1916
War Diary	Etree-Wamin	05/11/1916	05/11/1916
War Diary	Frevin-Capelle	08/11/1916	16/11/1916
Heading	War Diary 56 D.A.C. R.F.A. December 1916 Vol 15		
War Diary	Frevin-Capelle	01/12/1916	02/12/1916
War Diary	Auchel	03/12/1916	03/12/1916
War Diary	Haverskerque	06/12/1916	06/12/1916
War Diary	L.26.b.12	13/12/1916	28/12/1916
Heading	War Diary For January 1917 56 D.A.C Vol 16		
War Diary		02/01/1917	26/01/1917
Heading	War Diary 56th Div. Ammn. Col. February-1917 Vol 17		
War Diary		12/02/1917	26/02/1917
Heading	War Diary 56 D.A.C March 1917 Vol 18		
War Diary		01/03/1917	05/03/1917
War Diary	Calonne	07/03/1917	07/03/1917
War Diary	Witternesse	08/03/1917	08/03/1917
War Diary	Bergueneuse	09/03/1917	09/03/1917
War Diary	Boubers	10/03/1917	10/03/1917
War Diary	Grouches	13/03/1917	13/03/1917
War Diary	Lucheux	14/03/1917	14/03/1917

War Diary	Bavincourt	19/03/1917	19/03/1917
War Diary	Semincourt	19/03/1917	19/03/1917
War Diary	Bavincourt	18/03/1917	18/03/1917
Heading	56 Div Amm Col R.F.A. War Diary April 1917 Vol 19		
War Diary	Simencourt	01/04/1917	08/04/1917
War Diary	Agny	13/04/1917	29/04/1917
Heading	War Diary 56 D.A.C May 1917 Vol 20		
War Diary	Agny	02/05/1917	20/05/1917
War Diary	S.10.d.88	23/05/1917	31/05/1917
Heading	War Diary June 1917 56 D.A.C Vol 21		
War Diary	S.10.d.88	03/06/1917	03/06/1917
War Diary	S.8.A.5.1	27/06/1917	27/06/1917
Heading	War Diary 56 D.A.C RFA July 1917		
War Diary	S.8.A.51	01/07/1917	05/07/1917
War Diary	Coullemont	06/07/1917	06/07/1917
War Diary	Canettemont	07/07/1917	07/07/1917
War Diary	Croix	09/07/1917	09/07/1917
War Diary	Nedonchelle	10/07/1917	10/07/1917
War Diary	Neufpre	11/07/1917	11/07/1917
War Diary	D'Oxelaere	12/07/1917	12/07/1917
War Diary	Eecke	13/07/1917	13/07/1917
War Diary	Oudezeele	15/07/1917	29/07/1917
War Diary	Steenwoorde	30/07/1917	30/07/1917
Heading	War Diary 56 D.A.C R.F.A. August 1917 Vol 23		
War Diary	H.26.b.7.5	04/08/1917	24/08/1917
Heading	War Diary 56 D.A.C. September 1917 Vol 24		
War Diary	H.26.b.4.5	02/09/1917	02/09/1917
War Diary	Oxelaere	03/09/1917	03/09/1917
War Diary	Bapaume	04/09/1917	04/09/1917
War Diary	N.4.d.6.8	11/09/1917	15/09/1917
War Diary	H.35.c.Central	15/09/1917	17/09/1917
Heading	War Diary October 1917 56 D.A.C. R.F.A. Vol 25		
War Diary	H.35 Central	06/10/1917	27/10/1917
Heading	War Diary 56 D.A.C November 1917 Vol 26		
War Diary	H.35.c Central	01/11/1917	25/11/1917
Heading	War Diary December 1917 56 D.A.C R.F.A. Vol 27		
War Diary	H.35 Central	01/12/1917	14/12/1917
War Diary	Courcelle-Le-Conte	15/12/1917	15/12/1917
War Diary	Couves	16/12/1917	16/12/1917
Heading	War Diary Jany 1918 56 D.A.C. R.F.A.		
War Diary	Anzin	01/01/1918	15/01/1918
War Diary	Gauchin-Legal	21/01/1918	16/02/1918
War Diary	Anzin	27/02/1918	28/02/1918
Heading	War Diary 56 D.A.C February 1918		
Heading	War Diary 56th Divisional Ammunition Column R.F.A. March 1918		
Heading	War Diary 56 D.A.C. R.F.A. March 1918 Vol 30		
War Diary	Anzin	28/03/1918	28/03/1918
Heading	56th Divisional Artillery 56th Divisional Ammunition Column R.F.A. April 1918		
War Diary	Anzin	02/04/1918	02/04/1918
War Diary	F.22.d.6.0	08/04/1918	08/04/1918
War Diary	Montenes Court	14/04/1918	14/04/1918
War Diary	Simencourt	20/04/1918	24/04/1918
Heading	War Diary 56 D.A.C R.F.A. May 1918 Vol 32		
War Diary	Simencourt	01/05/1918	05/05/1918

War Diary	Montenescourt	19/05/1918	24/05/1918
Heading	War Diary 56th Div. Ammn. Column June 1918 Vol 33		
War Diary	Montenescourt	09/06/1918	22/06/1918
Heading	War Diary 56 D.A.C. July 1918 Vol 34		
War Diary	Montenescourt	01/07/1918	22/07/1918
Heading	War Diary 56 D.A.C. August 1918 Vol 35		
War Diary	Gauchin-Legal	01/08/1918	01/08/1918
War Diary	Montenescourt	22/08/1918	23/08/1918
War Diary	Le Fermont	24/08/1918	29/08/1918
Heading	War Diary September 1918 56 D.A.C. Vol 36		
War Diary	S.11.c.4.4	01/09/1918	04/09/1918
War Diary	T.2.d. Cent	05/09/1918	05/09/1918
War Diary	T.28.b.9.8	06/09/1918	06/09/1918
War Diary	T.2.D. Centl	07/09/1918	07/09/1918
War Diary	N.15.A.Centl	09/09/1918	30/09/1918
Heading	War Diary 56 D.A.C. R.F.A. October 1918 Vol 37		
War Diary	O 28 C.Central	01/10/1918	08/10/1918
War Diary	V 14.Central	08/10/1918	18/10/1918
War Diary	Rum & Court	20/10/1918	20/10/1918
War Diary	Morenchies	23/10/1918	23/10/1918
War Diary	Iwuy	30/10/1918	30/10/1918
Heading	War Diary 56 D.A.C November 1918 Vol 38		
War Diary	Haulchin	01/11/1918	04/11/1918
War Diary	Aulnoy	06/11/1918	07/11/1918
War Diary	Saultain	09/11/1918	09/11/1918
War Diary	Onnezies	11/11/1918	26/11/1918
Heading	War Diary December 1918 56 D.A.C. R.F.A. Vol 39		
War Diary	Onnezies	01/12/1918	04/12/1918
War Diary	Ciply	12/12/1918	01/04/1919
War Diary	Hyon-Ciply	06/04/1919	19/05/1919
War Diary	Jemappes	25/05/1919	28/05/1919

100 95/2041/1

56TH DIVISION

282ND (C. OF L) BDE RFA
FORMERLY 1/3 LONDON BDE
~~MAR - DEC 1918~~
1915 OCT - 1916 DEC

I ARMY

(MISSING 1916 OCT)

56 DIV TROOPS

ATTACHED 36 DIV

1/3rd London Bde R.F.A.
~~1915 Oct 1100 1915~~ DEC

1915 OCT — 1916 FEB

2293

56

1/3 London Bde
R.F.A

Vol V

282 BDE RFA

1/3RD LONDON BRIGADE
No
31 AUG 1915
— R. F. A. —

56 DIV

WAR DIARY
✱✱✱✱✱✱✱✱

Framlingham,
SUFFOLK.
31st. August 1915.

UNIT   1/3rd. London Brigade R.F.A.

DIVISION   58th. (London) Division

MOBILISATION CENTRE   London

TEMPORARY WAR STATION   Whitmoor Common

STATIONS SINCE OCCUPIED SUBSEQUENT TO CONCENTRATION :
        Maresfield Park, Dover, Rickmansworth, Wickham Market
        Framlingham.

(a) MOBILISATION   )   R E M A R K S :

(b) CONCENTRATION AT WAR STATIONS   )
        including Railway Moves   )

(c) ORGANISATION FOR DEFENCE   )
        including vulnerable points   )
)   NIL.
(d) TRAINING   )

(e) DISCIPLINE   )

(f) ADMINISTRATION   )

(g) RE-ORGANISATION OF T.F. INTO   )
        Home and Imperial Service   )

(h) PREPARATION OF THE UNITS   )
        for Imperial Service.   )

                                        Lieut:Colonel
                                        Commanding
                                        1/3rd. London Brigade R.F.A.

FRAMLINGHAM,
    Suffolk.

31st. August 1915.

121/74/32

(Attacks 36th Division) 36 DIV

1/3rd Bde: (London) R.7a.

Vol I

Oct 15
Nov 15

CONFIDENTIAL

WAR DIARY

of

1/3 LONDON BRIGADE R.F.A.

From 1st Oct to 31st Oct.

Army Form C. 2118

1/3 London Brigade R.F.A.

WAR DIARY
or
INTELLIGENCE SUMMARY
(Erase heading not required.)

Instructions regarding War Diaries and Intelligence Summaries are contained in F.S. Regs., Part II. and the Staff Manual respectively. Title Pages will be prepared in manuscript.

Place	Date 1915	Hour	Summary of Events and Information	Remarks and references to Appendices
Borden	Oct 1-3		Drawing stores for overseas	
	4		Left Borden for Southampton	
Havre	5		Arrived - Left same night	
			(horses)	
Argoeuves	6		Brigade Artillery training	
"	7,8,9		Inspection by G.O.C. 7th A.C.	
"	10,11,12		Brigade Artillery training	
"	13,14,15		Divisional training	
"	16		Brigade Artillery training	
"	17,18,19		March to Thièvres	
Sarly	20		Training with 48th Divisional Artillery	
"	21			
"	30		Marched to Thièvres	
Sèvres	31		Marched to Sèvres	

H. Fiszhes? Lt Col
C/1/3rd London Bde R.F.A.

WAR DIARY or INTELLIGENCE SUMMARY

Army Form C. 2118

Copy of Amend War Diary of 1/3 Lan Bde (282–1st Line) of Oct

Appendices folios

Instructions regarding War Diaries and Intelligence Summaries are contained in F.S. Regs., Part II. and the Staff Manual respectively. Title Pages will be prepared in manuscript.

(Erase heading not required.)

Place	Date	Hour	Summary of Events and Information	Remarks and references to Appendices
Baton	1–3		Drawing equipment in serve areas	
Southampton	4		Left Baton to Southampton	
Lion	5		Left Southampton shore	
Argoeuv	6		Arrived Lion & same night to Argoeuv	
"	7–19		Arrive Argoeuv	
"	20		Divisional Brigade and Battery training	
Thievres	21		Marched to Thievres	
Souly	22		Marched to Souly	
	23 (noon)		Gun drill. Laying out lines of communication to O.P. – 9" Battery Field/Rear	
			enemy trenches – See annex A	
"	23 (10am)		8" & 9" Batteries fired on enemy trenches (28 rounds) – See annex B	
"	24 "		7: 8: & 9" Batteries ditto (29 rounds) See annex C	
"	25 "		ditto (11 rounds) See annex D	
"	25 "		9" Battery	
"	26 "		7", 8" & 9" Batteries ditto (55 rounds Shrapnel 6 H.E.) See annex E	
"	27 "		8" & 9" Batteries ditto (25 rounds) See annex F	
"	28 "		7", 8" & 9" Batteries ditto (50 rounds Shrapnel 3 H.E.) See annex G	
"	29 "		7" 8" & 9" Batteries. B Bombardment (122 Shrapnel. 87 H.E.) See annex H	
"	30		Marched to Thievres	
Thievres	31		Marched to Heuu	

Signed,
1/3 Lan Bde RFA

Roll of Officers left behind with Details

10th Divn Amn Column

Bordon 2-10-1915

Rank	Name	Remarks
2 Lieut	F. O. Treckmann	

W. Hovenden Follett
LIEUT. COLONEL R.F.A.
COMMANDING 10TH DIVISIONAL AMMUNITION COLUMN.

Roll Officers proceeding Overseas.

10th Divn. Amn. Column.

Gordon   2-10-1915

Rank	Name	Remarks
Lt-Colonel	W. H. Ffolliott	
2/Lieut & Adjut	C. C. Stovas	
Captain	F. S. Upion Eckersall	
Captain	F. J. M. Dunne	
Lieutenant	M. J. Smith	
2/ Lieut	J. W. D. Fisher	
2/	J. W. Fennell	
2/	J. Blumer	
2/	J. S. Lyman	
2/	M. J. Spiers	
Lieutenant	F. J. Hunt. R.A.M.C.	

W. Hovenden Ffolliott
LIEUT. COLONEL R.F.A.
COMMANDING 10TH DIVISIONAL AMMUNITION COLUMN.

36th
to 38th 11.12.15

56 DIV

Confidential

1/3 London Bde RFA
Nov. Vol I A.

War Diary

of

1/3rd London Brigade R.F.A.

from 1st Novr 1915 to 30th Nov 1915

Army Form C. 2118

WAR DIARY
or
INTELLIGENCE SUMMARY
(Erase heading not required.)

Instructions regarding War Diaries and Intelligence Summaries are contained in F. S. Regs., Part II. and the Staff Manual respectively. Title Pages will be prepared in manuscript.

Place	Date Nov	Hour	Summary of Events and Information	Remarks and references to Appendices
Henu	19.5			
"	1		Battery training	
"	2		Battery training	
"	3		Battery training	
"	4		Battery training	
"	5		Battery training	
"	6		Brigade training	
"	7		Battery training	
"	8		Battery ranging in	
"	9		Battery - Horse show	
"	10		Battery training	
"	11		Brigade Reconnaissance	
"	12		Battery training	
"	13		Battery training	
"	14		Brigade training	
"	15		Battery training	
"	16		Battery training Reconnaissance	
"	17		Divine Service	
"	18		Divisional training	
"	19		Battery training	
"	20		Battery training	
"	21		Brigade Reconnaissance	
"	22		Buffalo training	
"	23		Battery training	
"	24		Divine Service	
"	25		Battery Training	
"	26		Battery Training	
"	27		Battery Training	
"	28		Brigade Training	
Mesnil	29		Battery Training	
"	30		Battery Training Advance party marched to Mesnil	
			Brigade marched Mesnil on change haves	
			Battery training	
			Battery training	

A.P.Mitchell 26/12
73rd Bde On Batt. RFA

attacks 36th

36th DIV

from 36th 11.12.15
to 47th 2.1.16.

1/3 London Bde R.F.A.
Dec
Vol II

2152

56 DIV

Attached 38 DIV

1/3rd London Bde R.F.A.

War Diary

Dec.

Army Form C. 2118

WAR DIARY
1/3rd LONDON BRIGADE. R.F.A.
INTELLIGENCE SUMMARY

(Erase heading not required.)

Instructions regarding War Diaries and Intelligence Summaries are contained in F.S. Regs., Part II. and the Staff Manual respectively. Title Pages will be prepared in manuscript.

Place	Date 1915 Dec.	Hour	Summary of Events and Information	Remarks and references to Appendices
MESNIL	1	—	Battery training.	
"	2	—	Brigade training.	
"	3	—	Divisional training.	
"	4	—	Battery training.	
"	5	—	Divine Service.	
"	6	—	Battery training — Brigade Ammunition Column moved to HOUDENCOURT	
"	7	—	Battery training.	
"	8	—	Battery training.	
"	9	—	Battery training.	
"	10	—	Battery training. Reformation for entraining at Station Marched to PONT REMY and entrained	
THIENNES	12	—	arrived at THIENNES	
"	13	—	Cleaning area	
"	14	—		
"	15	—	Battery training.	
"	16	—	Battery training.	
"	17	—	Preparation for change of station	
"	18	—		
"	19	—	Marched to FOSSE — Attached to 19th Divisional Artillery. Sector NEUVE CHAPELLE.	
FOSSE	20	—	— LA QUINQUE RUE. 7th Battery attached to 86 Bde R.F.A. 8th & 9th Batteries attached to 87th Bde R.F.A. Occupied gun positions — Ref. Map. FRANCE ("B." Series) Sheet 36 S.W. 1 - 20000 7th Battery S.1. a.2-3. 8th Battery M.31 a.3-5 9th Battery M.33. a.9 -c Ammunition Column - Ref. Sheet 36A S.E. 1 - 20000 2.30. b. 7-9	

1875 Wt. W593/826 1,000,000 4/15 J.B.C. & A. A.D.S.S./Forms/C. 2118.

WAR DIARY
1/3rd LONDON BRIGADE R.F.A.
INTELLIGENCE SUMMARY

Army Form C. 2118

(Erase heading not required.)

Place	Date 1915	Hour	Summary of Events and Information	Remarks and references to Appendices
FOSSE	21	—	Repairing Gun Epaulments	
"	22-23	—	9th Battery fired S. 39 rds. H.E 4 Total 39 . H.E 4	A
"	23-24	—	7th Battery fired S. 91 H.E 50. 8"Ballythien S. 37 - 9"Batty S. 58. H.E.14 " 186 . " 64	B & C
"	24-25	—	" " S. 60 H.E 40 8" " " . S 53 . 9" " S 141 . H.E. 7 . " 254 . " 47	D & E
"	25-26	—	" . S 138. H.E 104 8" " . S.3 L.H.E,9 " . S 128 . H.E. 24 . . " 297 . 139	F & G
"	26-27	—	" . S 66 H.E 8 8" " . S.22 H.E.26 9" " S 40 H.E 16 . " 128 . 50	H & I
"	27-28	—	" S 51 . H.E 38 8" " . S.59 H.E 9 " . S. 102 H.E. 3 . " 212 . 41	J & K
"	28-29	—	" S 56 . H.E.29 8" " S 76 H.E 42 9" S 55 H.E 6 . " 187. 47	L & M
"	29-30	—	Nil " S. 7.H.E 471 . 9" S . 38 - H.E 2 . " 45 . 73.	N & O
"	30-31	—	7th Battery - S. 24. H.E 125 - 8" " . S. 7. H.E 54 . 9. S . 190 H.E 2 . " 221 . 181	P & Q
			Ref. TRENCH MAP. Sheet 36. S.W.3. 1-10,000	
			On the 28th Dec 8"Howitzer over the zone S.11 a.5.5 ← S.11 a 0-2 from B Batty 87 'Ble R.F.A	
			1-9.167 M.35 α 9.3 to S.5.6.5-3 - D " R.H.A	
"	31st from noon		8' Battery fired S4. 14 H.E 54. 9'Batty S. 36 H.E. 12 40 . 66	R
"	31st		Withdrew from Gun Positions to Wagon line.	
			Total of Ammn expend. S/1609 H.E 712	
	31-12-15.			

Winchester Lt Col
1/3rd London Bde R.F.A

13rd. London Brigade, R.F.A.

Daily Report on Enemy Strong

12 Noon 23/12/15 to
12 Noon to 24/12/15

Hour	Nature of Gun.	Supposed Position of Gun.	Bearing of Flashes.	Position of Observer.	No. of Shell.	Locality Shelled.	Remarks
23.12.15 12.45.	5".9	Unknown	Unseen.	S.7.B.39	6.	S.1.D.	3 failed to explode

1/3RD LONDON BRIGADE
No
31 DEC. 1915
R.F.A.

1/3rd. London Brigade, R.F.A.

Daily Report on Enemy Artillery

12. Noon 24/12/15 to 12 Noon 25/12/15

Hour	Nature of Gun.	Supposed Position of Guns	Bearing of Flashes.	Position of Shell Observed.	No. of Shell	Locality Shelled.	Remarks.
11.45	Unknown	Unknown	Unknown	S7 B 39	7	S.1.D.	1 Failed to Explode.
1.30 p.m.	5.9	do.	do.	M.33.A.9.8. (Battery)	6	400 yards rear of Battery.	1 Short Burst. 1 Burst but smothered in mud & did not explode.
3.30 p.m.	15 pdr.	do.	do.	do.	8	200 yards left of Battery.	
5 am	15 pdr.	do.	do.	do.	8	100 yards right of Battery.	

1/3RD LONDON BRIGADE
No
31 DEC. 1915
R.F.A.

113rd. London Brigade. R.F.A.   G.   12 Noon 25/12/15 to 12 Noon 26/12/15

Daily Report on Enemy Artillery

Hour	Nature of Gun	Supposed Position of Guns	Bearing of Flash	Position of Observer	No. of Shells	Locality Shelled	Remarks
26.12.15 11 a.m.	Unknown	Unknown	Unseen	S.7.B.3.9	10	RICHEBOURG	
7.10 p.m.	15 pr.	"	"	M.33.A.9.8	3	About 500 yards N.E. Obelisk	One blind.
9.45 a.m.	do.	"	"	"	2	"	
5.45 a.m.	do.	"	"	"	12	"	

[Stamp: 113rd LONDON BRIGADE / 31 DEC. 1915 / R.F.A.]

113rd. London Brigade, R.F.A.

Daily Report on Enemy Artillery:— 12 Noon 26/12/15 to 12 Noon 27/12/15.

Hour	Nature of Gun.	Suspected Position of Gun.	Bearing of Flashes.	Position of Observer.	No. of Shells.	Locality Shelled	Remarks.
27.12.15 10.10	Unknown	Unknown	Unseen	S.7.c.39.	5	RICHEBOURG	

1/3RD LONDON BRIGADE
31 DEC. 1915
R.F.A.

1/3rd. London Brigade. R.F.A.

Daily Report on Enemy Artillery.

K

12 Noon 27/12/15 to
12 Noon 28/12/15.

Hour	Nature of Gun.	Supposed Position of Gun.	Bearing of Flashes.	Position of Observer.	No. of Shells.	Locality Shelled.	Remarks.
27/12/15. 11 am to 1.30 p.m.	5.9.	Unknown	Unseen	S.9.d.7.6	About 50	RICHEBOURG	Considerable damage done to church & adjacent bldgs.
12.10 p.m.	Centimetre 7.7	"	"	M.33.A.9.8.	" 12	M.34.C.7.3	
2.30 p.m.	7.7	"	"	"	" 10	M.27.D.5.0.6.	
3.0 p.m.	15 pr.	"	"	"	" 20	M.32.D.8.6.	

7/389 LONDON BRIGADE
31 DEC. 1915

1st Bat. London Brigade, R.F.A.   M   12 Noon 28/12/15 to
                                       12   29/12/15

Daily Report on Enemy Artillery:-

Hour	Nature of Gun.	Supposed position of Gun.	Bearing of Flash	Position of Observer.	No of Shells	Locality Shelled.	Remarks.
28.12.15. 2.30-to 3.30	4.2 & 5.9	Unknown	Unknown	S.9.d.7.7.	15	S.9.d.9.6.	3 Olive. Several direct hits on Factory.
28.12.15. 12.40 pm to 3.5 pm	15 Bursts	"	"	M.33.B.1.7½	1	S.9.A.6.9	Burst in air
	77	"	"	do.	1	M.33.A.9.6.	

1/89 LONDON BRIGADE
No   31 DEC. 1915
         R.F.A.

113rd London Brigade. R.F.A. From 12 Noon 29/12/15
To " 30/12/15

Daily Report on Enemy Artillery.

Hour	Nature of Gun	Supposed position of Gun	Bearing of Flash.	Position of Observer.	No. of Shells.	Locality Shelled	Remarks
29.12.15. 1.21 p.m. to 2.5 p.m.	5.9.	Behind Wortburg	Unseen	S.9.d.7.6	60.	O.P. on RUE DE BOIS.	15 Blinds
11.15 to 2.30	14. C.M.	Unknown	"	S.10.b.06.	15	S.10.b.06.	The number of Shells fired is approximate (all reports)
30.12.15 10.15 a.m. to 11.52.	7.7 CM	"	"	M.33.A.98	6	M.33.B.44	(1 Huge Blue Shell)
	—	"	"	"	2	do.	

13RD LONDON BRIGADE
No.
31 DEC. 1915
R.F.A.

1/Bde. London Bde. R.F.A. From 12 Noon 30/12/15 to 31/12/15.

Daily report on enemy artillery. — Q

Hour	Nature of Gun.	Supposed position of Gun.	Bearing of Flashes.	Position of Observer.	No. of Shells.	Locality Shelled	Remarks.
30.12.15 from 1.30 p.m. to 3.0 p.m.	77ª 5.9	BOIS DU BIEZ	Unknown	Sq. d. 7. 6.	60	Factory + Whisky Corner	
3.30. p.m.	77ᶜ	Unknown	Unknown	Sq. d. 7. 6.	4	S. 9. a. 5. 8.	
12.30. p.m	150ᶜ	Unknown	Unseen	M.33. a. 9.8	about 10.	M 34 c 75.	Hits on a house.
11.5. a.m.	77.	Unknown	Unseen	M.33. a.9.8	12	M 33 t. 5. 3.	(Three did not explode).

17/828 LONDON BRIGADE
No
31 DEC. 1915
R. F. A.

113rd London Brigade R.F.A.

Daily Report on Enemy Shelling 12 Noon 31/12/15 to 12 Noon 1/1/16.

S

Hour	Nature of Gun	Supposed Position of Guns	Bearing of Flashes	Point of Observer	No. of Shell	Locality Shelled	Remarks
31.12.15 3 p.m to 3.10 p.m	4.7 cwt.	Unknown.	Unseen.	M 33 a 9.8	about 20.	M.33. b.2.6	

1/113rd LONDON BRIGADE
No
31 DEC. 1915
R.F.A.

1/3rd. London Bde. R.F.A. "A"

Report on our Artillery

12 Noon 22/12/15" to
12 Noon 23/12/15"

Hour	Nature of Gun.	Battery firing & Nature in action	No. of Shell	Locality shelled	Position of Observer.	1. Report on effect of Fire. 2. Report on quality of Ammunition.
3.20 p.m.	18 pr. Q.F.	9th. London Bty. M.33.A.9.8	27 Rds. Shrap. (No. 80. Fuze.) 4 Rds. H.E	S.S.B.50	S.S.B.1.1½	1. Fire effective. 2. Ammunition good.
10.30 a.m.	do.	do.	12 - Shrap.	T.7.D.2½.6.	do.	do.

1/3RD LONDON BRIGADE
No
31 DEC. 1915
- R. F. A. -

1/3rd. London Brigade, R.F.A.   B.

Daily Report on our Artillery

12 Noon 23/12/15 to
12 Noon 24/12/15.

Hour.	Nature of Gun.	Battery firing & position in action	No. of Shell	Locality shelled.	Position of Observer.	
23.12.15. 12.30 p.m. to 1.30 p.m.	18 pdr. Q.F.	7th. London Battery S.7.B. 39.	41 Shrapnel	S.16.C.7.9½.	S.9.D.8.6½.	1. Report on effect of fire. Satisfactory. 2. Report on quantity of Ammunition. No.
24.12.15. 11.10 a.m. to 11.45 a.m.	do.	do.	50 " 50 H.E.	T.19.C.19	do.	1. do. 2. do.
23.12.15 2 p.m.	do.	8th. London Battery M.31.B.3.3.	34 Shrapnel	S.17.a.9.2	S.9.d.7.7.	1. Fire for registration purposes. 2. Good.
23.12.15 12.44 p.m. 1.20 " 1.53 " 2.5 " 2.20 " 2.30 "	do.	9th. London Battery M.33.A.9.8.	22 Shrapnel 6 H.E. 8 H.E. 17 Shrapnel 13 Shrapnel 6 Shrapnel	S.5.B.4½.0. S.5.B.4½.1. S.5.B.4½.1. S.5.B.9.0½. S.6.A.3.2. S.5.D.8.4½.	S.5.B.1.1½.	1. Fire effective. 2. Ammunition good.

1/3rd London Brigade, R.F.A.

12 Noon 24/12/15 –
12 Noon 25/12/15

Daily Report on our Artillery

Hour	Nature of Gun	Battery firing & position in action	No. of Shell	Locality Shelled	Position of Observer	1. Report of effect of fire. 2. Report on quality of Ammunition.
24.12.15. 5 pm to 7 pm	18 pdr Q.F.	7th London Battery. S.7.B.39	20 Shrapnel 10 H.E.	S.16 Central S.16. B.10.2		
25.12.15. 1 am	do.	do.	10 Shrapnel 20 H.E.	S.17a.45. to S.17.a.99.		1 Premature.
5 am to 7 am	do.	do.	30 Shrapnel 10 H.E.	S.16. Central to S.16. B.10.2.		
12.20 pm 24/12/15 to 3.30 pm	do.	8th London Battery M.31. C. 33.	53 Shrapnel	S.17.a. 92 & S.10.d. 53	S.9.d.7.7.	1. Good 2. Satisfactory
12.1 pm	do.	9th London Battery M.33. A. 9. 8.	13 Shrapnel	S.6. A. 3. 2.		
3.3	do.	do.	19 "	S.6. A 3. 2.		
3.10	do.	do.	24 "	S.6. C. O. 38		
3.50	do.	do.	12 "	S.6. C O 28.		
6.20	do.	do.	9 "	S.12. B. 7.7.		
6.23	do.	do.	1 H.E.			
1. 5 am	do.	do.	32 Shrapnel	S. 12. B. 7. 7.		
1.15	do.	do.	32 "	T.7.D.3. 32		

3rd London Brigade, R.F.A.   F   12 Noon 25/12/15 to
Daily Report on our Artillery.   12 Noon 26/12/15.

Hours	Nature of Gun	Battery firing & position in action	No. of Rd.	Locality Shelled	Position of Observer	Report on effect of Fire. Report on Quality of Ammunition.
25.12.15. 11.50 am. to 1.15 pm.	18 pr. Q.F.	7th. London Battery S.7.B.3.9.	45 Shrapnel 6 H.E.	S.16.A.77. S.16.A.78. S.16.D.77.6. S.16.D.98.	S.9.D.7.6.	1. Satisfactory. 2. Do.
5 pm. to 11 pm.	"	do.	20 Shrapnel 10 H.E.	S.16. (Central to) S.16.C.10.2.	do.	
26.12.15 - 1 am.	"	do.	10 Shrapnel 20 H.E.	S.17.A.45.63 S.17.a.99.	do.	
5 am. to 7 am.	"	do.	30 Shrapnel 10 H.E.	S.17.B. Central to S.16.B.10.2.)	do.	
9.45 am. to 12 Noon.	"	do.	33 Shrapnel 58 H.E.	Registration of Target.	do.	1. Good. 2. Nupo turning weak.
25.12.15. 1.35 pm. 2 pm.	"	8th. London Battery M.31.b.33.	31 Shrapnel 11 H.E.	S.17.a.82. S.10.d.63.6 S.11.c.25.	S.9.A.77	
2.25 pm.	"	"		S.10.d.63.6 S.16.B.96		
25.12.15. 3.45 pm. 4.10 5.50 pm.	"	9th. London Battery M.33.A.9.8.	12 Shrapnel 20 H.E. 6 Shrapnel 4 H.E. 12 Shrapnel	S.5.B.45.03 S.G.C.O.3½. 7.7.D.2.5½.		1. Effective 2. Good.
7.10 pm. 9.45 pm. 15 am.	"	"	8 12 8 14 6	S.12.B.7.7.5½ 7.Y.D.2.5½ S.12.B.7.7. 7.Y.D.2.5½ S.12.B.7.7		One Premature H.E.

1/3rd London Brigade, R.F.A. — H

Daily Report on our Artillery
12 Noon 26/12/15 to 12 Noon 27/12/15

Hour	Nature of Gun	Battery firing & Position in Action	No. of Shells	Locality Shelled	Position of Observer	Report on effect of Fire. Quality of Ammun.
26.12.15. 12.30 to 1/pm.	18 Pdr. Q.F.	S.Y.B.39. 7th. London Bty.	24 Shrapnel 4 H.E.	S.16.b.9.1½ to S.17.a.0½.3.	S.9.D.7.6.	1. 2.
3.15 pm to 3.45"	do.	do.	40 Shrapnel 2 H.E.	S.16.b.8.1½.	do.	
27.12.15. 11.25am to 11.35 "	"	"	2 Shrapnel 2 H.E.	S.16. D.7.7.	"	
26.12.15. 12.35 to 12.50	"	8th. London Bty. M.31. F.33.	4 Shrapnel 5 Shrapnel	S.10.d.64 to S.11.e.76. S.10.Ry.63.16. S.16.b.97.½.	S.9.d.77.	1. Good. 2. Satisfactory.
2.15pm to 3pm.	"	do.	25 H.E. 6 Shrapnel 1 H.E. 7 Shrapnel	S.17a.10.5. S.17a.77.		
26.12.15. 2.15 pm.	"	9th. London Bty. M.33. A.9.8.	20 " 6 HE 6 Shrapnel	S.6.A.3.1 T.8.B.3.3		
4.10 pm	"	do.	6 HE 6 Shrapnel	T.8.B.3.1		
4.12 "	"	"	4 H.E.			
1.30 am.	"	"	8 Shrapnel	T.2.B.8.4½.		

1/3RD LONDON BRIGADE
No
31 DEC. 1915
R.F.A.

1/3rd. London Brigade, R.F.A. J   12 noon 27/12/15
to 12 noon 28/12/5

Daily Report on our Artillery.

Hour	Nature of Gun.	Battery firing & Rotation in Action	No. of Shells	Locality Shelled	Position of Observer	Report on effect of fire. Quality of Ammn.
27.12.15 12.45 to 1.25.	18/pr Q.F.	S. 7. B. 39. 1/1st Co. /3 London Battery	17 Shrapnel	S 16 k 12 to S 16 k 32	S.9.d.7.6.	1. Report on effect of fire. Satisfactory 2. Quality of Ammn. Satisfactory
2.15 to 3.15.	"	"	12 " 26 H.E.	LORGIES	"	
28.12.15. 9.27 to 10.15.	"	"	22 Shrapnel 12 H.E.	S 16 C. 7.9.	"	
27.12.15 1.35 to 3 pm	"	M. 31 A 33 1/8. Co. of London Battery	36 Shrapnel	S. 12. C. 13.	S. 10. b. 16.	1. Good. 2. Fuzes burned Satisfactory
3.35 to 4 pm	"	"	15 "	S. 11. A. 72.	"	
28/12/15. 11.20 am to 11.25 am	"	"	8 "	S. 12. c. 13.	"	
12.44 hour	"	M. 33. A. 9. 8. 1/9 Co. /3 London Battery	102 " 3 H.E.	S. 5. B. 7.8.	M. 35. D. 4.1.	1. Effective 2. Ammunition Good.

1/3RD LONDON BRIGADE
No
31 DEC. 1915
— R.F.A. —

1/3rd. London Brigade R.F.A. From: 12 Noon 28/12/15.
To: 12 Noon 29/12/15.

L

Daily Report on our Artillery.

Hour	Nature of Gun	Battery firing & position in action	No. of Shells	Nature of Shells	Locality Shelled	Position of Observer	Report on effect of fire. — Quality of Ammn.
28.12.15 12 Noon – 12.10 12.25 – 1.55 pm	18 pr. Q.F.	7th London Bty. S.9.B.39 "	15 4 25 25	Shrapnel H.E. Shrapnel H.E.	S.17 Distillery do.	S.9.D.7.6 do.	1. Satisfactory 2. "
29.12.15 11 a.m. – 12.0	"	"	16	Shrapnel	S.16.a.7.8.	do.	
28.12.15 1.30 pm – 3.30. 10.40 am – 10.54	"	8th London Bty. M.37.B.3.3. do.	53 9 23 3	H.E. Shrapnel H.E.	S.11.d.5.6 to 39. S.11.d.56 to S.11.d.39.	S.10.E.1.6 do.	1. Good. 2. Satisfactory.
28.12.15 12.45 pm 3.35 pm. 7.5 pm.	" " "	9th London Bty. M.33.A.9.8. do. " "	12 13 12 4 18 2	Shrapnel " HE HE Shrapnel H.E.	M.35.D.10.2 S.5.B.7.8. S.12.C.0.3	M.35.D.3½.0½ M.35.D.4.7	1. Effective 2. Ammunition good, with exception Shrapnel — which is due to faulty primers.
29.12.15 7 am.		"			M.35.D.9½.2	M.35.D.3½.0½	

1/3rd. London Brigade. R.F.A. 12 Noon 29/12/15 to 12 Noon 30/12/15.

Daily Report on our Artillery.

Hour	Nature of Gun.	Battery Firing & Position in action.	No. of Shells	Locality Shelled	Position of Observer	1. Report on effect of Fire. 2. Report on quality of Ammn. & Ammn.
29/12/15 12.10 p.m.	18 pr. Q.F.	8th. Ldn. Bty. M. 31. B. 3.3	4 H.E.	S.11.a. 10.3	S. 10. b. 16.	Machine Gun emplacement damaged
2.35 p.m. to 3.30.	"	"	61 H.E.	S. 11. A. 2. 10 × S. 11. d. 10. 3	do.	On enemy's O.P. in retaliation for shelling our O.P.
8.21 p.m.	"	"	4 Shrap. 3 " 6 H.E	S. 11. a. 3.3 S. 12. a. 5.1	do.	Enemy's front line in retaliation for hostile anti-aircraft gun reported in action.
30/12/15 11.29 a.m.	"	"			Direct observation — Above inaccurate.	
29/12/15 3.30 p.m.	"	9th. Ldn. Bty. M. 33. A. 9.8	2 H.E. 21 Shrap.	S. 5. B. 5.2	S.5.B.0½.1½	Fuze and ammunition good. 1. Effective 2. Good (2 faulty primers)
7 p.m.	"	"	4 " 3 " 3 "	S. 6. A. 8. 8. S. 6. A. 5. 10. M. 36. C. 3.1	—	Ammunition good.
11.47 a.m.	"	"	7 "		—	1. Effective (wire cutting) 2. Good

1/3RD LONDON BRIGADE
31 DEC. 1915
R.F.A.

1/3rd Ldn Bde. R.F.A.   P

Daily Report on own Artillery

From 12 Noon 30/12/15 to 12" 31/12/15.

Hour	Nature of Gun	Battery firing & Position in action	No of Shells	Locality Shelled	Position of Observer	Report on effect of fire, quality of ammunition.
30.12.15 12.5 p.m. to 1.15 p.m.	18 pdr. Q.F.	4th C of London battery S.7. b. 3.9.	10 S 60 H.E.	Distillery and Earthworks S.16. d. 9.6	S.9.d.7.6	1. Report on effect of fire. Satisfactory. 2. " quality of ammunition. "
2.50 p.m. to 3.15 p.m.	"	"	13 H.E.	S.16. b. 5D	"	"
31.12.15 10.20 a.m. to 11.45 a.m.	"	"	14. S. 52 H.E.	S.16. c. 7.9½ S.16. b. 9.6 S.23. b. 5.2 S.16. a. 7.8	"	"
30.12.15 3 p.m. 3.5 p.m. 3.15 p.m. 31.12.15 11.5 a.m.	"	1/8 Co of London battery M.31. b. 3.3 " " " "	18 HE 24 HE 12 HE 1 S.	S.11. d. 4.7 S.11a.33 to S.10d.7.9 S.11. a. 33 S.11. d. 10.3	S.10. b. 1.6 " " "	A snipers post in "Hun House". Retaliation. Enemy machine gun emplacement. To find correction & error for the day.
30.12.15 12.1 p.m. 31.12.15 10.45 a.m. 10.30 a.m.	"	1/6 of London battery M.33. a. 9.8 " " "	143 S 41 S. 6 S. 2 HE	S.5. b. 7.8 S.6. a. 6½. 5 T.1. a. 5.1	N.35.D.5&0 S.5. a. 68½ "	Cutting lanes in wire. Effective. Ammunition good Registered guns on large mound. Effective. "

1/3RD LONDON BRIGADE
No
31 DEC 1915
R.F.A.

1/3rd. London Brigade. R.F.A.

Report on our Artillery

R

12 Noon 31/12/15 to 12 noon 1/1/16

Hour	Nature of Gun	Battery firing & Position in Action	No. of Shell	Locality Shelled	Position of Observer	1. Report on effect of Fire 2. " " quality of Ammunition
31.12.15						
2.15 p.m to 3.40 p.m	18 Pdr. Q.F.	1/5th Co. of London battery u. S. M 31. b 33	24 HE	S 10 d. 7.9 to S 11 a. 3.3	S. 10 b. 16	On enemy trenches in retaliation. 1. Effective. 2. Good
"	"	"	15. HE	S 11 a 6.1 to S 11 a. 9.3	"	
"	"	"	15. HE	S 11 d. 4.8	"	Hostile O.P. 1. Effective. 2. Good.
1.30 p.m.	"	1/4th Co. of London battery M 33 a. 9.8	12. H.E 36. S.	S 5 b 7½.5 to M 35 d. 8½.4	S. 5. a. 6.8½	1. Effective. 2. Good.

[Stamp: 1/3RD LONDON BRIGADE No 31 DEC. 1915 R.F.A.]

47TH DIVISION

1-3RD LONDON BRIGADE RFA
JAN-FEB 1916

1/3 London RFA.
Jan Vol II a.

Confidential

War Diary

of

1/3ʳᵈ LONDON BRIGADE R.F.A.

from 1ˢᵗ to 31ˢᵗ January 1916

47ᵗʰ
from 3E. 4ᵗʰ 2.1.16
to

1/3rd LONDON Brigade R.F.A

WAR DIARY
INTELLIGENCE SUMMARY

Army Form C. 2118

Place	Date 1916	Hour	Summary of Events and Information	Remarks and references to Appendices
FOSSE	Jany 1	—	Brigade moved from FOSSE to FAUCQUENHEM.	
FAUCQUENHEM	2		Brigade moved from FAUCQUENHEM to AMES	
AMES	3		Cleaning area and checking stores	
—"—	4		Battery training	
—"—	5		Inspection by G.O.C. R.A. IV Corps. Ammn Coln moved to FAUCQUENHEM	
—"—	6		Battery training	
—"—	7		Battery training	
—"—	8		Brigade less Ammn Coln moved to LIERES.	
LIERES	9		Service Adm - Divine Service R.C.	
—"—	10		Battery training	
—"—	11		Brigade reconnaissance - AUCHELL	
—"—	12		Battery training	
—"—	13		Battery training	
—"—	14		Exercise order - Inspection of Horses and Equipment	
—"—	15		Divine Service R.C.	
—"—	16		Battery training	
—"—	17		Battery training	
—"—	18		Battery training - G.O.C. in C.	
—"—	19		Battery training	
—"—	20		Battery training - Inspection of Harness & Equipment	
—"—	21		Inspection of Harness & Equipment	
—"—	22		Divine Service	
—"—	23		Passed through LIERES en rout to 47" Divn.	

1875 Wt. W593/826 1,000,000 4/15 J.B.C. & A. A.D.S.S./Forms/C.2118.

47th. Divisional Artillery - General Report
6.30 am. to 28/1/16 to 6.30 am 29/1/16.

Locality	Battery	Time	No. of Rounds fired Shrap.	HE	Target Engaged	Retaliation for enemy Shelling	Remarks
G.27. C.3.1	7th. Bty.	6.30 pm. to 6.30 am.	25	25	Night lines H.3.C.1.1½ M.6.C.5.7 M.6.C.8.8 M.6.C.4. & Working party M.6.B.2½.6.	By Order of Corps Group At request of Infantry	Ammunition Good.
		10.45 pm.	6				
		8.45 am.– 9.5	6				
		9.50 am.– 10.0 am	9		On Zero lines	Searching & Sweeping at irregular intervals.	
		11.5 am.– 11.15	7		" "		
		11.30.– 11.40	11		" "	At request of Infantry	
		1.5 pm to 1.30	20		" "		
G.27.C.11	8th. Battery	9.45 am.		110	M.5.C.9½.4 M.5.C.5.5 M.5.C.3.7 M.5.C.1.9	Consequent upon enemy mine being exploded left of Zone.	Continued until Infantry reported further fire was not required.
		10.33 am.	7		M.5.c.1.9.		Finding corrector
		4.15	26	12	Day lines.	In retaliation for Enemy Shelling O.P. with lachrymatory projectile	
G.27.C.11.	do.	10.5 pm.	4	4	M.5.C. M.5.C.37		Enemy Sap As ordered.
		12.15 am.	4	4			
		12.30	4	4			
		3.45	4	4			
		3.55	4	4			
		5.45	4	4			
G.27.C.12	9th. Battery	9.36	–	20	M.5.D.2½.4½ to M.5.D.9½.4	Our support trenches.	
		10.8	5	1	M.5.D.6½.6½.8	Error of the day & corrector	
		11.53	8	16	M.5.D.1½.6½ to M.5.D.6½.8	Retaliation.	
		1.2 pm	39	48	M.5.D.2½.4½ to M.5.D.9½.7 M.5.D.1½.6½ - M.5.D.6½.8	Our front & support trenches	Enemy ceased firing.
		2.55	–	8	M.5.D.2½.4½ to M.S.D.9½.7	Our support trenches.	do. do.
		3.5	–	7	M.5.D.7.9.	Registering new trench	
		3.10	–	7	M.5.D.3.9.	" "	

47th. Divisional Artillery - General Report.

6.30 a.m 29/1/16 to
" 30/1/16 D

Locality	Battery	Time	No. of Rds. fired. Shrap.	H.E.	Target Engaged	In retaliation for enemy shelling.	Remarks
27.C.3.1	7th. Battery	6.30 p.m. – 6.30 a.m.	38.	12	Night lines. M.3.c.1.1½. M.6.6.5.7. M.6.6.8.8. M.6.6.4.4.	By order of Love Group.	
do.	do.	10.45 to 11.10	9.	9	M.6.B.3.7 (Working party & new trench)	At Request of Liaison Officer	Party dispersed. Pointing out lines.
		3.15 p.m. to 3.20.	6.	4			
27/c.11	8th. Battery	11.30 a.m.	3.	18	M.5.C.8.½ night line	—	Zero line. Corrector & error of the day.
	do.	2.15 p.m.	31	3	M.4.d.77– M.4.6.9.3		Registration of SALIENT BARRAGE.
		3.10 p.m.	28.	12	M.5.d.7.4 M.6.c.7.7.		Registration of COPSE BARRAGE.
do.		8.50.	4	4	M.5.C.		Enemy sap as ordered.
		12 (Mid night)	4	4	M.5.C.37		
		3.30 a.m.	4	4	M.5.C.5.5		As Ordered.
		5.50	4	4			
27.C.12.	9th. Bty.	10.15	—	8	M.5.D.2½.4½	Our support trench	Called for by our Infantry.
		10.30.	—	18	M.5.D.9½.7½		
		11.0	10	—	M.5.D.1½.6½		Error of the day & corrector
		11.21	4	—	M.5.6.9.0		Registration
		11.35	—	2	M.5.c.7½.6½		Registration (Enfilade new trench)
		11.57	—	5	M.5.c.9.5.		Registration do. do.
		2.5 p.m.	—	7	M.5.D.4.5.		"Communication trench. (? Machine Gun emplacement)
		2.21.	3	13	M.5.D.9.2½.		Registration (Commn. trench front of house ? Officers HQ).

47th. Divisional Artillery - General Report.

Locality	Battery	Time	Number of Rds. fired Shrap.	H.E.	Target engaged	In retaliation for enemy shelling	Remarks
G.27.C.3.1	7th. Battery	8 p.m 29/1/16 6.30 am 30/1/16	48	-	LOOS Crassier Rly. x LOOS-ST. LAURENT ROAD. and M.6.6.3.6. new trench	At request of LOWE GROUP & Liaison Officer	
G.27.C.11	8th.	11.10 p.m. 11.25 " 12.55 a.m. 1.5 " 2.35 " 3.15 " 3.35 " 5.45 " 5.55 " 6.5 "	2 2 2 2 2 2 2 2 2 2	2 2 2 2 2 2 2 2 2 2	M.5.c. M.5.c.9.3		Enemy SAP As ordered.
G.27.C.1.2	9th.	11.30 to 11.50 p.m. 3.5 p.m 3.10 " 3.15 "	20 3	4 1 1 2	M.5.d.0.8 M.5.d.3.9; M.5.c.9.5½; M.5.c.9.4½; M.5.d.2½-5½ M.5.d.3.10.	SAP HEAD Communication trench Saphead.	By Order Registered yesterday
"	"	3.40 p.m	-	4	M.5.d.0.8 - M.5.d.6.9	New Trenches.	

47ᵃ
to 56ᵃ
21.2.18.
1/3 London Bde R.F.a
___
Fit
___
Vol III

1/3rd LONDON Bde R.F.A.

Army Form C. 2118

WAR DIARY
INTELLIGENCE SUMMARY

Place	Date 1916 Jan'y	Hour	Summary of Events and Information	Remarks and references to Appendices
LIEVRES	24		O/C + Unit Commanders proceeded to LES BREBIS.	
"	25		1 Sec. Each Battery moved to LES BREBIS.	
"	26		Brigade less Ammn Coln proceeded to LES BREBIS Ammn Coln HOUCHIN	A
LES BREBIS	27		Brigade attached to 47th Division. Batteries took on their positions occupied by 1st London Bde R.F.A. attached LOWE Group	B
"	28		Ditto	C
"	29		Ditto	D
"	30		Ditto	E
"	31		Ditto	

[signature] Lt Col
1/3 London Bde RFA

WAR DIARY / INTELLIGENCE SUMMARY

Army Form C. 2118

1/3rd LONDON Bde R.F.A.

Place	Date 1916 February	Hour	Summary of Events and Information	Remarks and references to Appendices
LES BREBIS	1st		Attached 47½ Divisional Artillery in the Line	See appendix A attached
	2		"	B
	3		"	C
	4		"	D
	5		"	E
	6		"	F
	7		"	G
	8		"	H
	9		"	I
	10		"	J
	11		"	K
	12		"	L
	13		"	M
	14		"	N
	15		"	O
	16		1 Section of each Battery withdrawn + positions taken by Sec/ns of 1st Division throughout NAMES	P
	17		Ditto	Q
	18		" Battery training	R
AMES	19		" "	
"	20		" "	
"	21		" "	
"	22		" "	
"	23		" "	
"	24		Marched to BERGUETTE for purpose of entraining. Headquarters, 7th Battery & 1/2 8th Battery. Brigade detrained at A 8th Battery, 9th Battery + Bde Amm. Col. PONTREMY	
Headquarters at CAUMONT	25		Arrival of Units at CAUMONT, LIMERCOURT, & LIMEUX	
FRANCIERES	26		Marched to FRANCIERES with 169th Infantry Brigade	
"	27		Battery training	
"	28			
"	29			

29.2.18 J. V. Reid Lt. Col.
Lt. Col. 1/3rd London Bde R.F.A.

47th Div. Arty.

The G.O.C. wishes me to express his appreciation of the excellent work done by the 47th Divisional Artillery and attached batteries during the last four days.

The calls on them for support have been continuous and in every case have been complied with smartly.

The continuous nature of their duty in supporting the infantry during the recent bombardment carried out as it has been under heavy shell fire and rendered the more arduous by lachrymatory and gas shells cannot but have been a very severe strain. The continuous night work in maintaining the supply of ammunition has also been severe.

The discipline and devotion to duty displayed has been admirable and worthy of all praise.

The G.O.C. wishes his appreciation and complete satisfaction with their efforts to be communicated to all ranks.

G/750/3

30th January 1916.

Lt. Colonel,
General Staff,
47th (London) Division.

The G.O.C. R.A. has much pleasure in forwarding the above remarks and once again heartily congratulates all ranks on the excellent services they have rendered.

B.M.732.

30/1/16.

Lieut. for
Brigadier-General Comdg.
47th. Divnl. Arty.

47th Divisional Artillery - General Report. 1/2/16 A.

ality	Battery	Time	Number of Rds. fired Shrap.	H.E	Target Engaged	In Retaliation	Remarks
7.C.3.1	7th. Bty.	6.30 pm 30/1/16 to 3.30 am 31/1/16	32		LOOS - ST. LAURENT Rd	Lowe Group	
"	"	4.30 to 6.30	39	83	German front line trenches	By request of Liaison Officer	
"	"	12.10 pm to 12.50	-	13	G.36.D.6.0 Barricade	Registration by Infantry	
"	"	2.0 pm to 2.25		30	G.36.D.6.0	Lowe Group	At 12.50 pm there was a premature in our right rear, but have not been able to ascertain Battery.
"	"	3.10 pm to 3.25	17	9	Front line trench	At request of Liaison Officer	
"	"	3.35 pm to 3.50	16	8	do. do.	do.	
7.C.11	8th.	6.35	4		- -	- -	Enemy Sap. Bombardment as ordered. Corrector for the day as ordered.
"	"	7.30 to 7.50	100	88			
"	"	12.5	9		Zero line		
"	"	2 pm		30	M.5.c.3.7		
"	"	3 pm	3	2	M.4.d.8.8 M.5.c.1½.7		
27.C.12	9th. Bty.	8.57		4	M.5.d.1½.6½ - M.5.d.6½.8½	Our front line	Request Infantry.
do.	do.	9.15		4	M.5.d.2.8	Forward Saphead	Registration
"	"	12.50 1.30		9	M.5.d.5.9½		"
"	"	1.56	6	-	M.5.d.2½.6½		
"	"	2.0		30	M.5.c.9.6	Road	By Order.
"	"	2.50	2	8	M.5.d.2.9½	Forward Saphead	Registration.
"	"	3.16	12	-	M.5.d.1½.6½ - M.5.d.6½.8½	Our front line	Retaliation
"	"	3.20	2	-	M.5.d.1½.6½		Test 85 fuze for Corrector.

47th Divisional Artillery - General Report   2/2/16

Locality	Battery	Time	Number of Rounds fired Shrap.	H.E.	Target engaged	In retaliation	Remarks
G.27.C.3.1	7th Battery	31.1.16. 7.30 pm to 7.55	100	101	German Front line & Support trenches in Zone	Special Orders from Group	
do	do	2.2.16. 4.30 am to 7.45	75	81	German Front line trenches in Zone	By request of Division on Offensive operation of our enemy front line trenches	
do	do	11.3 am to 11.55	33	5	G.36.d.68.0. Barricade	Registration	
		12.20 pm to 12.35	6				
		1.8 pm to 1.20	6	1	Mound West	At request of Infantry	
do	do	1.39 to 2.14	12	12	G.36.d.6½.0.		
		4.5 to 4.20 pm		10	New Sap M.6.B0-5½	Registration	
G.27.C.11.	8th Battery	2.10 to 4 pm	12	30	M.4.d.8.8	Registration of CASSIER & COPSE	
			19		M.5.d.	Barrage	
G.27.C.11	8th Battery	9.19 pm		4			
		11.30		4			Sap Head
do	do	2.45 am		2			as required
		5.30		4	M.5.c.		by Infantry
		6.0		6			
do	do	12.10		2			8 Trench
		12.25		2			ordered
		4.25		2			
G.27.C.12.	9th Battery	12.45 pm	2	-	M.5.d.1½.8½		Time over
do	do	1.31 pm	-	7	M.5.a.8½.8	Sap Head	Repulse
do	do	1.48	-	8	M.5.d.5½.9½	Mound Sap	
do	do	2.46	-	12	M.5.d.3.9	Sap Head	
do	do	3.2	-	19	M.5.d.4.9	"	
do	do	3.28	-	13	M.5.d.10.3	Fortified House	Effective aiming

47th Divisional Artillery – General Report. 2/2/16.

C

Locality	Battery	Time	Rounds of Ble Fired Shrap.	HE	Target Engaged	Remarks
G.27.c.31.	7th Bty.	1.2.16 6.30 pm to 7.30 am		14	Saps. M.L.B.O. 5th Working party	In retaliation
		9.4 am to 9.7		6	M.L.B. 7.9	At request of Liaison Officer
		3.30 am to 3.40		14	Day line	At request of Liaison Officer. Notification of Day line. (Mountain gun Major)
G.27.c.11	8th.	12 - 10 pm 2-10 pm	8 11	1 23	Zero line Knoogen	
"	"	"	5	6	Barrage	
"	"	10.15	4	5	Copse Barrage M.S.C.	Sap head.
"	"	11.45	-	2 19	"	By request of Infantry
"	"	12.30 am	-	2		
"	"	1.12	-	2		

C

3.16	"	2	
3.40	"	2	
3.50	"	2	
4.10	"	2	
4.30	"	2	
4.45	"	2	
5.10	"	2	
5 am	"	2	
G.27.c.12.9th. 11	4	M.S.d. 1½.6½-6	o"Out front line Enemy's fire ceased.
		M.S.d. 1½.6½-8½	n" " Trenches To find correction & error
11.50	5	M.S.d. 1½-6½	" of the day.
12.1 pm			
12.10 "	10	M.S.d. 2½-4½	" To find correction & error
		M.S.d. 9½-7	" of day.
	12	M.S. d. 10-3	"
2.50 "	8	M.S.a. 5½-9½	laghead Fortify House.
2.55 "	8	M.S.a. 3.9	— " "
3 pm	9	M.S.a. 9½.8	— Effective.

47th. Divisional Artillery — General Report   4/7/16 D.

Locality	Battery	Time	Number of Rounds fired Shrap.	H.E.	Target Engaged	Elevation	Remarks
G.21.c.3.1	7th Battery	6.20/am 2/7/16 6-20am 3/7/16	47	1	M.6. 4.2½ . 9		By request of Liaison Officer. Another party am.
"	"	9.15 & 6.31 9.20am 7/7/16		4	M.6. & 7.4½		By request of Liaison Officer.
"	"	10.2.50am to 11.38	6		M.6. 6½. 3½ Wastering parts.		"
"	"	12.30am 6.5pm 16 1.10 —	2	1	-do-		"
"	"		5	1	Loos Barrage		By order of Corps Genl.
G.21.c.11.	8th "	11.30 a.m. 2.25 pm 4 pm	5 9 10	2 28 25	Zero line M.S.C. Salient Barrage		Orders from Brigade. Retaken by Enemy.
G.21.C.12	9th "	11.36 a.m. 11.39 " 3.35 pm	2 —	6 11	M.S.D.4.3. M.S.D.4.3. M.S.D.6.B. 2		Retaken by (No Map) To find correction Line of Sight. Answered a letter in Editor Memoir.

8/1/16 E

47th Divisional Artillery. — Gunner Report.

Locality	Battery	Time	Rds. fired Shrapnel	H.E.	Target Engaged	In Retaliation	Remarks
G.27.c.3.1	7th Bty.	11.20 pm	4		N.6.b.32. Working party on sap.	At request of Liaison Officer.	Correction for the day.
G.27.c.11.	8th.	10.30 am to 10.40	4	35	LOOS BARRAGE		Registration of LOOS BARRAGE.
do.	do.		16		M.5.c.		Enemy sap as others.
do.	do.	6.30 am to 6.30 am	90		M.11.a.9½.5 to M.11.c.5½		Enemy sap as others. Transport on road to
do.	do.	7.20 am	15	1	M.5.d.3.7.		Post no. 11
G.27.C.1.7	9th. Bty.	10.35	2	1	M.5.8.3½	Fire corrects & 2nd Nah Head	Post no. 11 Effective.
do.	"	10.40	—	7			
do.	"	11.45	—	8	M.11.R.2.4½	—	Enemy's O.P. (Man seen (Henry.))

47th Divisional Artillery - General Report 10/1/16   F

Locality	Battery	Time	Number of Rds. Fired Shrap.	H.E.	Target Engaged	In Retaliation	Remarks
G.27.C.3.1	7th.	8.30 pm 4/1/16 to 6.15 am 5/1/16	6		M.6.6.7.4.	At request of Liaison Officer	Reported by telephone & Telegraph at 7. am. 5.2.16.
		5.2.16 2.15 pm. to 2.30 pm.	10	2	Day line	Registration	
		4.5" to 4.20"	7				
G.27.C.1.1	8th.	11.30	1	8	2000 line M.5.c.8.2½	—	Wiring party
do		8.15	4		" Night line		"
do		8.45	4		" "		"
		5. am			M.5.d.16.6½		do
G.27.C.12	9th.	10.33.	1				To find corrector & Elev. for the day.
		12.40		22	M.11.6.2.4½		Germany O.P. window Fired to take out surrounding wall

47th Divisional Artillery - General Report.

7/2/16
G.

Locality	Battery	Time	Number of Rds. fired Shrap.	H.E	Target engaged	In Retaliation	Remarks
G.27.c.3.1	7th.	9.0pm 7/2/16 to 6.0am 8/2/16	50	30	As ordered	By order of Corps Group.	
		11.45am to 12.15pm	11	2	M.6.d.29	Front line trenches occupier	To check range
		3.10 to 3.12 pm	2	1	M.6.b.72	Our Periscope in accordance with F.J.L.7	Reported by 2Lt. Howitzer.
G.27.c.11.	8th.	10.11 to 10.29	4	16	Enemys O.P.		Fuse 11 & Corrector for the day.
G.27.c.12.	9th.	10.0am	2	–	M.5.d.7.3		Topped corrector & error of the day.
		11.0am	–	7	M.11.b.2.4½		German O.P. (Observer withdrawn)
		2.35pm	10	7	M.5.d.0.2½		Registering enemy's new forward trench stops.
		6.30	4	4	M.5.d.8½.4	As ordered	
		7.5	4	4	"		Enemy new forward trenches.

47th Divisional Artillery - General Report.   H

Locality	Battery	Time	Number of Rds. fired Shrapnel	H.E.	Target engaged	In retaliation	Remarks
7.C.3.1	7th. Bty.	7th. 6.0 am to 7.0 "	7	-	M.6.d.2.9	At request of Infantry on Sap	Result appeared satisfactory.
do.	do.	10. Am to 10.20	-	9	M.6.d.2.9		
do.	do.	2.45 pm to 3.5 pm	1	30	M.6.d.3.9½ M.6.b.6.5½ M.6.c.8.7½ N.1.a.4.5½	Registration from line trenches	
7.c.11	8th.	11.17 am to 12.25 pm	3	-	Night Lines & CROSSVER BARRAGE		To corrector for day. Verification.
do	do.	2.43 to 3.11	1 6	12 12	M.5.D.		Registration of Sap outside Zone in case fire required at Midnight
do.	do.	6.30 am 6.30 pm.	37 39	13 12	Tgt. S. Tgt. T.		
2.a.7	9th.	11.5 am	9	-			To find error of the day & corrector.
do	do.	2.40 "	-	5	M.5.d.4½.4½		Saphead
do	do.	2.42 pm	-	3	M.11.b.9.7		Fortified House.
		3.41 "	-	3	M.5.c.9½.3		Saphead.

47th. Divisional Artillery - General Report.

9/2/16

Locality	Battery	Time	Number of Rds. fired Shrapnel	HE	Target Engaged	In Retaliation	Remarks
G.27.c.3.1	7th. Battery	9.50 a.m. 10.0 a.m.	4	1	Day Lines		Obtaining Corrector & Error for day.
G.27.c.1.1	8th.	4.20	36	25	Night Lines.		
G.33.d.3.7	9th. Bty.	10.28 a.m.	1	-			Obtain Corrector & Error of day.
		11.34	-	4	M.5.d.5.4½ (D.dugout - Maj. Clifton's sketch.)		Cpl. Stead.
		11.44	-	5	M.5.c.9½.3. (H.E.dugout - Maj. Clifton's sketch.)		" "
		2.5.	-	9	M.11.b.9.7		Fortified House.

27th. Divisional Artillery – General Report. 10/2/16

Locality	Battery	Time	No. of Rds. fired Shrap.	H.E.	Target Engaged	For Retaliation	Remarks
27.c.3.1	7th. Bty.	6.30pm to 8.20am	50	50	LENS ROAD M.b.d.27	By orders Corps H.Q.	
		12.30pm to 12.40	4		M.6.d.29	Obtaining correction Corrector day	
		2.45 to 2.50	8		Front line Trenches	At request of Division Officer	
27.c.1.1	8th.	2.17pm to 2.7		26 11	Alight house & M.11.a.6.9		Fine of day in preparation for bombardment
		3.20		30 10			Bombardment as ordered
		4.5		30 10			
		4.40		30 10			
27.c.1.1	do.	9.05pm		8	Tgt. L		
		12.10 am		8			
		3.40		12			To find corrector & error of day Snipers House registration
33.a.77	9th. Bty.	10.45 am 11.2	1 4	3	M.6. c.6.2		
35.d.39	9th. Bty.	2.45 pm	–	4	M.5.c.29 to M.u.d.3.4		Registration
do.	do.	3.20	–	10	do do		Effective in Trench & entrance tunnel.
do.	do.	4.5	–	10	. .		
do.	do.	4.40	–	10	. .		

11/2/16 K.

47th Divisional Artillery - General Report.

Locality	Battery	Time	No. of Rds. fired Shrap.	H.E	Target engaged	In Retaliation	Remarks.
G.27.c.3.1	7th Bty.	10/2/16. 2.55 pm to 3.25 pm.	11	10	Day Line		—
G.27.c.1.1	8th "	2.30 " to 3.50 "	5	6	Zero line.	Instructional	Corrector for the day. Enemy O.P.
do.	" "	Nil	Nil	17	Three 11.		
G.3.3.C.27	9th "	11.55 am.	2	1	M.11.R.9.7		To find corrector & error of day. Fortified House.
		1. pm.	1	8	M.5.d.5.4½		Sab Head.
		2.15 "	1	5	M.5.A.3.2		Moat Line trench.
		2.20 "	1	4			

47th. Divisional Artillery - General Report

12/2/16

Locality	Battery	Time	No. of Rds Fired Shrap.	H.E.	Target engaged	On Retaliation	Remarks
7.C.3.1	7th. Bty	11/2/16 12.55 pm to 1.5 "	3	2	Day lines.	Obtaining error for day.	
"	" "	2.35 " to 4.5 pm.	16	4	M.6.b. 3½ . 4	Registration at request of liaison Officer.	Observation interrupted as another battery firing on same target.
7.C.1.1.	8th.	7.15 am.	3	—	Road at M.18.a.		As ordered.
do.	" "	12.5 to 12.45	11	—	Night Lines.		Corrector for the day.
"	" "	12.55 to 1.29	9	7)	Hose 11.		Static O.P.
"	" "	3.30	4	—)			
"	" "	4.6 to 4.14	—	8)			
3.3.C.2.7	9th. "	10.37 am	2	—			To find error & corrector for day. Machine guns emplacement. Emplacement in by our fire & a great deal of timber displaced. Considered important registration.
"	" "	11.30 "	—	15	M.15.d.7.3 (Ref. Major Clifton's sketch) Enemy's front line trench mid way & immediately south of letters D & C.		
3.3.C.2.7	9th. Bty	2.55 am.		14	M.5.d.1.0 (Ref. Major Clifton's sketch) Immediately behind benches in enemy's front line trench between road & letter G.		Ruined house Suspected M.G. emplacement. Shells burst no dug out or —

47th Divisional Artillery - General Report

M 12/2/16

Locality	Battery	Time	Rounds Fired Shrap.	Rounds Fired H.E.	Target Engaged	Observation	Remarks
G.27.c.3.1	7th Bty.	11/2/16 7.45 p.m.	2		N.7.c.9.1.	By others & own Flash	
do.	"	12/2/16 2.0 a.m. 5.30	12	5	M.6.D.2.9.	do.	
do.	"	9.55 a.m. to 10.0	5		Front line trenches	Obtaining correct fuse for day.	
do.	"	10.25 to 10.30 a.m.	5				
"	"	6.15 p.m. 6.30	20		M.L.A. 2.9.6 M.C.B. 4.0 M.11.B.1.32.	At request of Liaison Officer.	
G.27.c.11.	8th.	9.5 a.m. 7.20 p.m. 11.30 "	13 15	Sgt. S.T.			To find corrector for day. Also on M.5.c.x 9.
"	"	10.45 to 11.45 7.35 a.m.	7 8 7				Fired at M.18.a. as ordered.
"	"	4.0 5.0	1				
G.32.c.27	9th.	10.3	1				To find error & corrector for day.

14/2/16

47th Divisional Artillery - General Report.

Locality	Battery	Time	No. of Rds. fired H.E. Shrap.	Target Engaged	Elevation	Remark
G.27.c.1.1.	8th. Battery	10.5 p.m.	8.	Zero Line. Night.		For correction for day.
do.	do.	7.2 a.m. 8.20 9.30	11. 3. 3.	Zero line + M.S.C. 5.1.		Suspected new enemy work.
		12.1 a.m. 9.45	4.	House 1.1.		Working party.
G.33.c.2.7	9th. Bty.	11.26 " 2.35 p.m.	11.	M.5. d. 8. 4½ (old lines marked coll wire) Major Clifton Kerr		To find correctors & errors of day. Reps. Ahead.

O 18/2/16

47th Divisional Artillery — General Report.

Locality	Battery	Time	Number of Rds. Fired Shrap.	H.E.	Target Engaged	In retaliation	Remarks
G.27.c.3.1	7th. Bty.	14/2/16. 7.10 a.m. to 7.50 a.m.	28		Night Lines	Retaliation on "Moving up" of mine	Reported by telephone to S.O.M.E. Show 12.30 a.m. 14-2-16. Enemy mine exploded.
G.27.c.1.1	8th Bty.	6.45 to 7.25	40		Zero line		
"	"	10.5 a.m.	1				
"	"	12.10 to 2.55	24		Covert Tgt.		
"	"	2.50-2.57	6		Night Lines		
"	"	3.24	1		Covert		
"	"	3.27	2		Night		
"	"	3.37	1		Covert		
"	"	3.52 to 4 p.m.	4		Night Covert		
"	"	3.5 to 4 p.m.		68			
G.33.c.27	9th. "	9.55 a.m.	4	4	M.S.d. 9.4.4.		To find error & correction for stray shots. Registration M.G. Emplacement.
"	"	10.3 "		7	M.S.d. 7.3		
"	"	1.15 p.m.					

16/7/16 P.

47th Divisional Artillery - General Report.

Locality	Battery	Time	Number of Rds. fired Shrap.	H.E.	Target Engaged	In Retaliation	Remarks
G.27.C.3.1	7th Bty.	15/7/16 11.30 a.m. to 11.40 a.m.	9	-	M.G.D. 26.9 to M.G.B. 4.4.	At request of Infantry	Result appeared Satisfactory.
G.27.C.11	9th "	10.10 to 10.19 3.0. 3-28	8 22	-	Zero Line "Roost" Tgt Target		
" "	" "	8.15 a.m. to 5.10 a.m.	30	31	Tgt. 7.8. Tgt. S.		As Ordered & as required by Infantry.
G.33.C.2.7.	9th "	10 a.m. 2.45 p.m.	2 -	9 8	M.S.d.8.4.4. M.S.d.16.3½		To find effective range of day. Definite Advanced Trench no. no.

47th. Divisional Artillery - General Report. 11/2/16.

Locality	Battery	Time	Number of Rds. fired. Shrap. / H.E.		Target Engaged.	In Retaliation	Remarks
G.27.c.3.1	7th. Bty.	-	-	-	-	-	-
G.27.c.1.1	8th. "	11.16 am to 11.33	10	-	Fosse 11	-	To obtain corrector for the day. The shortest range of FOSSE 11
G.33.c.27	9th. "	1.10 pm - 3.30	3	7 4	M.5.d.8.1½. M.5.c.9b.3.	-	Advanced trenches Saphead

47th Divisional Artillery - General Report. 18/5/16.

Locality	Battery	Time	Number of Rds. fired Shrap.	H.E.	Target Engaged	In Retaliation	Remarks
G.27.c.3.1.	7th Bty.	10.15 to 10.30.	5	3	Day fire	Obtaining corrector & error for day	
G.33.c.27	Ditto "	12.29 pm - 1.5 pm	— 1	13 —	M.12.a.1½.7½		Notified House. Smoke seen rising therefrom. No fresh corrector for the day.

Army Form C. 2118

WAR DIARY
or
INTELLIGENCE SUMMARY
(Erase heading not required.)

Instructions regarding War Diaries and Intelligence Summaries are contained in F. S. Regs., Part II. and the Staff Manual respectively. Title Pages will be prepared in manuscript.

Place	Date MARCH	Hour	Summary of Events and Information	Remarks and references to Appendices
FRANCIERES	1.		BATTERY TRAINING.	
	2.		do.	
	3.		do.	
	4.		BRIGADE DRILL ORDER.	
	5.		BATTERY TRAINING.	
	6.		do. UNIT COMMANDERS ATTENDED INFANTRY DEMONSTRATION ADVANCE.	
	7.		DIVINE SERVICE.	
	8.		BATTERY TRAINING.	
	9.		do.	
	10.		BATTERY DRILL ORDER. 8th. BATTERY DEMONSTRATION TO INFANTRY COMMANDERS.	
	11.		BATTERY TRAINING.	
	12.		CHANGE OF STATION. ARRIVED AUTHEUX.	
AUTHEUX	13.		BATTERY TRAINING.	
	14.		ditto. AMMN. COLUMN HORSES INSPECTED BY C.R.A.	
	15.		ditto.	
	16.		CHANGE OF STATION - ARRIVED BOURET - SUR - CANCHE.	
BOURET SUR CANCHE	17.		BATTERY TRAINING.	
	18.		GUNDRILL - AMMN. COLUMN. BATTERY TRAINING.	
	19.		DIVINE SERVICE. OFFICERS RECONNAISANCE.	
	20.	9-4	BRIGADE TRAINING.	
	21.		BATTERY TRAINING. AMMN. COLUMN - GUN DRILL.	
	22.		BATTERY DRILL ORDER.	
	23.		BATTERY TRAINING.	
	24.	9-4	BRIGADE TRAINING.	
	25.	9-12	RECONNAISSANCE - AMMN. COLUMN - ROUTE MARCH.	
	26.		DIVINE SERVICE.	
	27.	9-4	BRIGADE TRAINING.	
	28.		BATTERY " do. EXERCISE ORDER - GUN DRILL.	
	29.		BATTERY TRAINING.	
	30.	9-4	BRIGADE TRAINING.	
	31.			

Signed,
LIEUT. COLONEL
COMMANDING
1/2nd LONDON BRIGADE R.F.A.

31 MAR 1916

WAR DIARY
or
INTELLIGENCE SUMMARY

(Erase heading not required.)

Army Form C. 2118

Instructions regarding War Diaries and Intelligence Summaries are contained in F.S. Regs., Part II. and the Staff Manual respectively. Title Pages will be prepared in manuscript.

Place	Date April	Hour	Summary of Events and Information	Remarks and references to Appendices
BOURET	1		Demonstration of Infantry attack (Trench warfare) under cover of smoke cloud.	
"	2		Divine Service.	
"	3		Battery Training 9am to 1pm - cleaning up village - Officers Reconnaissance.	
"	4		Officers Reconnaissance.	
"	5		Battery Training and Brigade Reconnaissance	
"	6		Brigade Training 9am. 4pm.	
"	7		11 am. Inspection by G.O.C., R.A. II Corps.	
"	8		Divine Service - FLAMMENWERFER Demonstration.	
"	9		Brigade Training and Test of communications.	
"	10		Battery " 9am to 4pm.	
"	11		Brigade " "	
"	12		Battery "	
"	13		" " Inspection of Matériel and equipment.	
"	14		Divine Service. C.O. proceeded on course at 3rd Army H.Q. - New Battery joined and designated "R" Bty.	
"	15		Battery Training.	
"	16		" "	
"	17		" " Visit of Unit Commanders to positions in the line.	
"	18		" "	
"	19		" "	
"	20		" " C.O. returned from course at 3rd. Army. H.Q.	
"	21		" " LECTURE to all Officers by C.O.	
"	22		Divine Service. 9am.	
"	23		Brigade Training 9am. to 4 pm.	
"	24		Battery "	
"	25		" " visit of C.O. and Battery Commanders to positions in the line.	
"	26		" "	
"	27		" "	
"	28		Brigade Training 9am. to 4 pm.	
"	29		Battery Training and Inspection.	
"	30		Divine Service 9am.	

30/4/16

[signature] R. Ruddle
LIEUT COLONEL
COMMANDING
1/3rd LONDON BRIGADE R.F.A.

Army Form C. 2118

WAR DIARY
or
INTELLIGENCE SUMMARY
(Erase heading not required.)

282ND. BRIGADE
No
31 MAY 1916
— R.F.A.

Place	Date MAY	Hour	Summary of Events and Information	Remarks and references to Appendices
BOURET-SUR-CANCHE	1.	6am.	BRIGADE and BATTERY TRAINING.	
do	2.		do.	
"	3.		do.	
"	4.		do.	
"	5.		do.	
"	6.		do.	
"	7.		CHANGE OF STATION – Brigade Headquarters at SOUASTRE & Brigade Wagon Line at PAS.	
SOUASTRE	8.		BATTERY TRAINING at PAS.	
"	9.		do.	
"	10.	✱	do.	✱ Brigade Designated 282nd. Bde. R.F.A.
"	11.		VISIT of C.O. to LINE with C.R.A.	
"	12.		" " " and BC's. to LINE to select positions	
"	13.		DIGGING GUN POSITIONS, DUG OUTS, AMMUNITION MAGAZINES &c. in environs of HEBUTERNE – Wagon Line at PAS.	
"	14.		do.	
"	15.		do.	
"	16.		do.	
"	17.		do.	
"	18.		do.	
"	19.		do.	
"	20.		do.	
"	21.		do.	
"	22.		do.	
"	23.		do.	
"	24.		do.	
"	25.		do.	
"	26.		do.	
"	27.	✱	do.	✱ D/282 Battery Transferred to 253rd. Bde. R.F.A. but attached to 282ND Bde. R.F.A for tactical purpose. Rendezvous. C/283 Battery posted to 1/282np (Londonderry) Bde, but attd. as D'Bty. till June.
"	28.		do.	
"	29.		do.	
"	30.		do.	
"	31.		do.	

[signature] LIEUT. COLONEL
COMMANDING
282ND. BRIGADE R.F.A.

Army Form C. 2118

282nd BRIGADE, R.F.A

WAR DIARY
or
INTELLIGENCE SUMMARY
(Erase heading not required.)

Vol 7

Place	Date June	Hour	Summary of Events and Information	Remarks and references to Appendices
SOUASTRE	1.		All Batteries excavating and constructing Gun positions, OP's & at HEBUTERNE, Wagon Line at P'is	
	2.		do.	
	3.		do.	
	4.		do.	
	5.		do.	
	6.		do.	
	7.		do.	
	8.		do.	
	9.		do.	
	10.		do.	
	11.		do.	
	12.		do.	
	13.		do. Wagon line moved to HENU.	
	14.			
	15.		Wirecutting Group - A/282, B/282, C/282, C/283, A/280, D/280	
	16.		B/282 Registering first 50 A, 21 AX.	
	17.		" " 105 A.	
	18.		Batteries A/282 31 A. — C/282 31 A — D/280 40 B.X.	
	19.		" 68 A, 2 A.X. — B/282 46 A. — C/282 23 A — C/283 15 A — D/280 47 B.X.	
	20.		" 91 A, " — C/282 8 A. 32 A.X. — D/280 44 B.X.	
	21.		C/282 32 A. — C/283 33 A. 10 A.X. — D/280 53 B.X.	
	22.		C/283 9 A.X. — B/282 16 A. — C/282 65 A — D/280 42 B.X. Powder Shell 1.	
	23.		C/282 31 A — C/283 31 AX. — D/280 46 B.X. Powder Shell 3	
HEBUTERNE	24.		Wirecutting commenced in front of enemy's trenches. Ammunition Expended	
	25.		do.	
	26.		do.	
	27.		do.	
	28.		do.	
	29.		do.	
	30.		do.	

	A/282		B/282		C/282		C/283		A/280		D/280	
	A	A.X.	A	A.X.	A	A.X.	A	A.X.	A	A.X.	B	Bx Powder
	558	-	205	-	197	-	302	144	207	-	120	3
	1028	-	750	65	1254	-	404	-	592	-	216	-
	818	-	1195	-	1057	-	545	-	766	-	293	-
	573	-	1077	7	584	-	973	8	666	-	256	-
	677	-	1389	18	649	-	647	-	758	-	30	-
	437	8	261	25	800	-	512	-	522	8	149	-
	427	2	457	-	509	9	444	-	690	15	-	-

LIEUT COLONEL
COMMANDING
282nd BRIGADE R.F.A

ORIGINAL

Army Form C. 2118

WAR DIARY
of
INTELLIGENCE SUMMARY 282nd Brigade R.F.A.
(Erase heading not required.)

Vol 3

Instructions regarding War Diaries and Intelligence Summaries are contained in F.S. Regs., Part II. and the Staff Manual respectively. Title Pages will be prepared in manuscript.

Place	Date 1916 July	Hour	Summary of Events and Information	Remarks and references to Appendices
			Reference Map FONQUEVILLERS Sheet 57 D NE Scale 1/2.	
HEBUTERNE	1		Supporting attack on GOMMECOURT.	
"	2		Covering Infantry Holding Line	
"	3		"	
FONQUEVILLERS	4		Battle H.Q. moved to FONQUEVILLERS (E.26 a 9.4) covering from K.3.d.6.7. to E.23.c.7.7. held by 168th Infantry Brigade.	
"	5		Supporting 168th Infantry Bde.	
"	6	6pm	168th Infantry Bde relieved by 169th Infantry Bde. Group reconstituted. Batteries B/280 C/280 D/280 joined Group.	
"	7		Supporting 169th Infantry Bde	Batteries A/123. B/123 D/123 joined Group
"	8		"	
"	9		"	→ A/123 B/123 D/123 left Group and rejoined 37 Division
"	10		"	
"	11		"	C/263 B/280 C/280 left the Group
"	12		"	
"	13		"	Zone covered E.28.d.6.9 to E.28.b.6.4.
BIENVILLERS	14		Battle H.Q. moved to BIENVILLERS (E.8.a.90.85) B/280 and D/282 joined Group. D/280 left Group.	
"	15		"	
"	16		"	Zone covered E.28.b.30.28 to E.11.c.6.9
"	17		"	C/282 left Group & joined Centre Group. B/282 covered E.28.b.80.36 to E.11.b.60.50
"	18		"	
"	19		"	
"	20		"	

Army Form C. 2118

WAR DIARY
or
INTELLIGENCE SUMMARY
(Erase heading not required.)

Instructions regarding War Diaries and Intelligence Summaries are contained in F.S. Regs., Part II. and the Staff Manual respectively. Title Pages will be prepared in manuscript.

Place	Date 1916 July	Hour	Summary of Events and Information	Remarks and references to Appendices
BIENVILLERS	21		Supporting 169 Infantry Bde.	
"	22		"	
"	23		Zone covered E.28.c.30.28 to E.5.d.45.20.	
"	24		" " " " " "	
"	25		" " " " " "	
"	26		" " " " " "	
"	27		" " " " " "	
"	28		" " " " " "	
"	29		" " " " " "	
"	30		" " " " " "	
"	31		" " " " " "	

Pickell Lt Col
c/ 282 Brigade R.F.A.

56th Divisional Artillery.

282nd BRIGADE

ROYAL FIELD ARTILLERY.

AUGUST 1 9 1 6

ORIGINAL
282nd Brigade, R.F.A.   Army Form C. 2118

Vol 9

WAR DIARY
or
INTELLIGENCE SUMMARY

(Erase heading not required.)

Instructions regarding War Diaries and Intelligence Summaries are contained in F.S. Regs., Part II. and the Staff Manual respectively. Title Pages will be prepared in manuscript.

Place	Date Aug. 1916	Hour	Summary of Events and Information	Remarks and references to Appendices
BIENVILLERS	1		Supporting 149th. Infantry Brigade.	
	2		,,	
	3		,,	
	4		,,	
	5		,,	
	6		,,	
	7		,,	
	8		,,	
	9		,,	
	10		,,	
	11		,,	
	12		,,	
	13		,,	
	14		,,	
	15		,,	
	16		,,	
	17		,,	
	18		,,	
	19		,,	
	20		149th. Infantry Brigade relieved by 51st. Infantry Brigade, 17th. Division.	
	21		Supporting 51st. Infantry Brigade. Batteries A/280, B/280, A/282, B/282, D/282.	
	22		,,	
	23		,,	
	24		,,	
	25		,,	
	26		1 Section of B/282 relieved by a section of 17th. Divl. Artillery.	
	27		1 Section of B/282 relieved by section of 78th Brigade, R.F.A.	
	28		Relief completed of B/280, A/280, A/282, D/282 by 17th Divl. Artillery.	
	29		Relief of B/282 completed. Command of Group assumed by relieving Group. 9 Battery Commanders. Headquarters & Batteries to PAS.	
	30		At PAS.	
	31			

NOTE:- From 2nd to 15th Aug. GROUP H.Q. was relieved by Brigade H.Q. 280th. Brigade, R.F.A.

Mulls
Lt. Col.
Commanding 282nd. Brigade, R.F.A.

1875 Wt. W593/826 1,000,000 4/15 J.B.C. & A. A.D.S.S./Forms/C. 2118.

56th Divisional Artillery.

282nd BRIGADE R. F. A.

SEPTEMBER 1916.

Army Form C. 2118

WAR DIARY
or
INTELLIGENCE SUMMARY
(Erase heading not required.)

282nd Brigade, R.F.A.

Vol. 6

Place	Date 1916.	Hour	Summary of Events and Information	Remarks and references to Appendices
PAS	September 1.		Preparations for departure - Detached PAS 2hr. and arrived LE MEILLARD same day.	On action in SOMME OFFENSIVE from 5/9/16 onwards.
LE MEILLARD	2.		Battery training and preparation for departure.	
"	3.		Detached LE MEILLARD and arrived AILLONVILLE.	
"	4.		AILLONVILLE and arrived DOUARS.	
DOUARS.	5.		" DOUARS and arrived BRAY SSOMME - moved into action in SOMME District.	
	6.		In action at A.S.c. 8.3 - REF. FRENCH MAP GUILLEMONT 1/20,000, parts of SHEETS 57c S.W. and 62c N.W.	
	7.		Advanced to new positions at B.7.c.6.6.	
	8.		In action at do	
	9.		do at do	
	10.		do do	
	11.		do do	
	12.		do do	
	13.		do do	
	14.		do do	
	15.		do do	
	16.		do do	
	17.		do do	
	18.		do do	
	19.		Advanced to new positions at T.20.d.3.2.	
	20.		In action at do	
	21.		do do	
	22.		Advanced to new positions at T.25.c.90.15.	
	23.		In action at T.25.c.90.15.	
	24.		do do	
	25.		do do	
	26.		do do	
	27.		do do	
	28.		Moved into new positions S.E. of MORVAL in T.16.a and T.15.b.k.a.	
	29.		In action at above.	
	30.			

Alfred O'Connor
Lieut. Colonel
Commanding 282nd Brigade, R.F.A.

Vol 12

War Diary. November. 1916.

282nd Brigade RFA.

(ORIGINAL)

ORIGINAL

WAR DIARY
or
INTELLIGENCE SUMMARY
(Erase heading not required.)

Army Form C. 2118

282nd Brigade R.F.A.

Instructions regarding War Diaries and Intelligence Summaries are contained in F.S. Regs., Part II and the Staff Manual respectively. Title Pages will be prepared in manuscript.

Place	Date Nov. 1916	Hour	Summary of Events and Information	Remarks and references to Appendices
MAMETZ	1		Departed MAMETZ and arrived at DOUARS.	
DOUARS.	2		" " DOUARS " " MOLLIENS.	
MOLLIENS.	3		" " MOLLIENS " " AMPLIER in the ORVILLE DISTRICT.	
AMPLIER.	4		" " AMPLIER " " BOURET - SUR - CANCHE	
BOURET.	5		" " BOURET " " LARESSET. Brigade re-organised into 2 - 18pdr. 6 gun Batteries and one 4.5" How. 4 gun Battery. One section of each Battery relieved 301st. Fd. RFA. - Can. Div. Arty.	
G.Q.G.	6		Relief completed - Supporting 8th. Canadian Infantry Brigade.	
	7		" " " " "	
	8		" " " " "	
	9		" " " " "	
	10		" " " " "	
	11		" " " " "	
	12		" " " " "	
	13		" " " " "	
	14		" " " " "	
	15		" " " " "	
	16		" " " " "	
	17		" " " " "	
	18		" " " " "	
	19		" " " " "	
	20		Successful bombardment carried out in support of raid carried out by the Infantry at 12.30 a.m. on night of 20/21.5. The How. Battery knocked out a Machine Gun Emplacement.)	
	21		Supporting 8th. Canadian Infantry Brigade.	
	22		" " " " "	
	23		" " " " "	
	24		" " " " "	
	25		" " " " "	
	26		" " " " "	
	27		" " " " "	
	28		" " " " "	
LARESSET.	29		Relief commenced by 9th. Canadian Artillery Brigade, C.F.A. - On night of 30 t. Nov. 1st. Dec.	
	30		" completed " 9th. " " "	

J. Berry Nott?
for Lieut. Colonel.
Commanding
282nd Brigade, R.F.A.

WAR DIARY

Vol 13 282nd Bde RFA. December 1916

(ORIGINAL)

WAR DIARY
or
INTELLIGENCE SUMMARY 282ND Brigade, R.F.A.

(Erase heading not required.)

Army Form C. 2118

ORIGINAL

Place	Date 1916	Hour	Summary of Events and Information	Remarks and references to Appendices
LARESSET	Dec 1		At Wagon Line LARESSET preparing departure.	
	2		Departed LARESSET and arrived RAIMBERT LES AUCHEL.	
	3		RAIMBERT and arrived HAVERSKERQUE.	
	4		HAVERSKERQUE and arrived LAVENTIE.	
LAVENTIE	5		One section each 18 Hd. Battery relieved a section of 2 Lt. & 3rd. Batteries 6th. Div. Arty.	
	6		Relief completed – both 18 Hd. Batteries in action also 500 H. How. Bty. – D/282 remained in rest.	
	7		Supporting 169th. Infantry Brigade. 282nd. Bde. H.Q. called Right Group with A/282, B/282, C/282 & 109H. Battery	
	8		do. do.	
	9		do. do.	
	10		93rd Battery joined Right Group.	
	11		do.	
	12		Relief of 169th. Infantry Brigade by 168th. Infantry Brigade.	
	13		Supporting 168th. Infantry Brigade.	
	14		Bombardment of enemy's trench junction carried out.	
	15		do. do.	
	16		Brigade Headquarters relieved by 280th. Brigade, R.F.A. Headquarters – 282nd. Headquarters for rest.	
	17		B/282 Battery relieved by A/280 Battery – B/282 Battery at rest in Wagon Line.	
	18		A/282, C/282, & D/282 Batteries in Right Group. Group H.Q. 280th. Brigade, R.F.A. – 282nd. Brigade H.Q. at rest.	
	19		ditto do.	
	20		do. do.	
	21		D/282 Battery with the C.O. & 6 Signallers at Headquarters in Left Group, 37th. Division.	
	22		do.	
	23		do.	
	24		Relief commenced by Battery of 37th. Divc. Arty.	
	25		" completed " 37th. Divc. Arty.	
	26			
	27			
	28			C.O. and 6 Signallers returned.
	29			
	30			
	31			

E. Brown
for LIEUT. COLONEL
COMMANDING 282nd. BRIGADE R.F.A.

10095/29412

BEF
56 DIV

283 Bde RFA

formerly 1/4 LOND Bde

1915 OCT — 1916 SEP

BROKEN UP 15.11.16
(see Oct Diary)

2502

56 DIV TROOPS

ATTACHED 36 DIV
1/4d London Bde. R.F.A
Oct - Nov 1915.

2293

283 BDE RFA 58 DIV

UNIT:- 1/4th, LONDON HOWITZER BRIGADE.

BRIGADE:- DIVISIONAL ARTILLERY.

DIVISION:- 1st, LONDON DIVISION.

MOBILIZATION CENTRE:- Headquarters,
Ennersdale Road,
Lewisham, London, S.E.

STATIONS SINCE OCCUPIED
SUBSEQUENT TO CONCENTRATION:- Whitmoor Common;

Maresfield Park;

Redford Barracks,
COLINTON,
Midlothian, N.B.

East Grinstead, SUSSEX;

Ipswich (In billets);

Warren Heath Camp, Ipswich.

TEMPORARY WAR STATION:- Warren Heath Camp, Ipswich.

-o-o-o-o-o-o-o-o-o-o-o-o-o-o-o-o-o-o-o-o-

STATEMENT TO ACCOMPANY WAR DIARY FOR AUGUST? 1915.

(d). TRAINING:- Training has been carried out during the past month in accordance with weekly Training Programme. Musketry Exercises and Minature range Practices.

A Draft of Officers, N.C.O's and men of the 2nd., Line have been attached for a course of training during the whole of the month. This has been carried out satisfactorily.

A detachment of Infantry have commenced a course of Transport Duties. Instruction is being giving in Riding, Driving, and Stable management.

(e). DISCIPLINE. The Discipline of the Brigade on the whole is very good.

(f). ADMINISTRATION.

(1). Medical Service:- There has been a slight amount of Diarrhoea and stomach trouble, otherwise little or no illness, and the health on the whole is very good.

(2). VETERINARY Services:- Excellent - Special precautions have been taken against Mange and Ringworm with complete success.

(3). SUPPLIES:- An A.S.C. Supply Depot has now been established in the Camp. Its service is very good.

(5). **ORDNANCE.** Not yet satisfactory. Stores are still due on outstanding Requisition.
One Limber and Wagon Body is still due from "Repairs" Woolwich, since last October.

(9). **SUPPLY OF REMOUNTS:-** Good. A steady supply during the month, but still many below Establishment.

GENERALLY.

The condition of the Unit on the whole is good. New harness has been secured by both Batteries and Ammunition Column and now brought into use. Many of the Remounts are unbroken and therefore require Schooling.

Brigade Headquarters has received a Telephone Wagon, but for the want of Stores, Harness and necessary Telephone and Signalling Equipment for same, is at present useless.

Lt.-Col. R.F.A.(T).
Commanding I/4th, London Howitzer Brigade.

--------oooOoooo--------

Warren Heath Camp,
    Ipswich.

31st, August, 1915.

Army Form B 234.

FIELD STATE.

Unit 1/4th LONDON HOWITZER BRIGADE (Including Bde & Batteries of 4" How Bde RFA)

Place Gordon Camp

Date 27/9/15

To be rendered in accordance with Field Service Regulations, Part II.

UNIT	FIGHTING STRENGTH												RATION STRENGTH									
	Personnel		Horses and Mules		Other Animals	Guns and Ammunition Wagons (stating nature)	Machine Guns	Ambulances	Tool Carts, Technical Carts (stating nature)	Remarks		Personnel	Horses and Mules		Other Animals	Mechanically Propelled Vehicles					
	Officers	Other Ranks	Riding	Draught and Pack								Total, all Ranks entitled to Rations	Heavy Horses	Other Horses and Mules		Motor Cars	Motor Bicycles	Lorries		Tractors	Remarks
																		3 Ton	30 Cwt.		
(1)	(2)	(3)	(4)	(5)	(6)	(7)	(8)	(9)	(10)	(11)	(12)	(13)	(14)	(15)	(16)	(17)	(18)	(19)	(20)	(21)	(22)	(23)
1/4th London Howitzer Brigade	22	645	209	453			4·5 Q.F.B.L. Howitzers 16			13	Rifles 165	680	8	669								1 Maltese Cart 5 Gotho Carts 5 Mules 1 G.S. Wagon 1 Telephone Wagon
						Royal Wagon Limbered 32			6	Pistols											¾ Horses in B & C Batteries for 4 G.S. Wagons for First Transport Attached
						Ammun Wagons 16															
TOTALS																						

Ammunition with Unit:—
·303 inch; approximate number of rounds per Man 50
·303 inch; ,, ,, ,, per Machine Gun
Gun or Howitzer; approximate number of rounds per Gun or Howitzer Nil

Supplies with Unit:—
Approximate number of days' rations for men of ration strength 1
,, ,, ,, forage for Animals
,, ,, ,, fuel and lubricants for Mechanically Propelled Vehicles

Signature of Commander _Chas A Scroll_ Capt. R.F.A.
Adjt. 1/4th London Howitzer Brigade

Army Form B 231.

Unit 1/2nd. LONDON BRIGADE R.F.A.
Place BORDON
Date 27/9/1915.

FIELD STATE.

To be rendered in accordance with Field Service Regulations, Part II.

This should not include details attached to unit, or personnel detailed to march with the Train, or any men unfit to go into action with unit.

To include Fighting Strength, Personnel detailed to march with the Train, and all Personnel and animals attached for Rations and Forage

UNIT	FIGHTING STRENGTH											RATION STRENGTH							
	Personnel		Horses and Mules		Other Animals	Guns and Ammunition Wagons (stating nature)	Machine Guns	Ambulances	Tool Carts, Technical Carts (stating nature)	Remarks	Personnel	Horses and Mules		Other Animals	Mechanically Propelled Vehicles				Remarks
	Officers	Other Ranks	Riding	Draught and Pack							Total, all Ranks entitled to Rations.	Heavy Horses	Other Horses and Mules		Motor Cars	Motor Bicycles.	Lorries 3 Ton	Lorries 30 Cwt.	Tractors
(1)	(2)	(3)	(4)	(5)	(6)	(7)	(8)	(9)	(10)	(11)	(12)	(13)	(14)	(15)	(16)	(17)	(18)	(19)	(20)	(21)	(22)	(23)
1/2nd. LONDON BRIGADE R.F.A.	19	623	190	399			12-Guns 18pr.QF 24 Wagons 18pr.Q.F. 19 Wagons G.S. 7 Carts S.A.A.			4* 4ø 1x 1+	Rfls. Bi-cycles 160 5	649	591									*Carts water. ø; cooks x Cart Medl. Equip. + Cart Telephone

Totals ...

Ammunition with Unit:—
.303 inch; approximate number of rounds per Man
.303 inch; " " " per Machine Gun
Gun or Howitzer; approximate number of rounds per Gun or Howitzer

Supplies with Unit:—
Approximate number of days' rations for men of ration strength
" " " forage for Animals
" " " fuel and lubricants for Mechanically Propelled Vehicles

Signature of Commander

[signed] LIEUT.-COLONEL
COMMANDING 1/2ND LONDON BDE R.F.A

Army Form B 231.

FIELD STATE.

Unit _1/3rd LONDON BRIGADE R.F.A._
Place _Gordon, Hants._
Date _24 Sept. 1915_

To be rendered in accordance with Field Service Regulations, Part II.

FIGHTING STRENGTH

This should not include details attached to unit, or personnel detailed to march with the Train, or any men unfit to go into action with unit

UNIT	Personnel		Horses and Mules		Other Animals	Guns and Ammunition Wagons (stating nature)	Machine Guns	Ambulances	Tool Carts, Technical Carts (stating nature)	Remarks
(1)	Officers (2)	Other Ranks (3)	Riding (4)	Draught and Pack (5)	(6)	(7) (8)	(9)	(10)	(11)	
Headquarters Staff	3	37	28	7					X	Rifles (12) Bicycles
do A.V.C.	1	1								
do A.S.C.		12								
do R.A.M.C.	1	4								
7th Battery	4	141	44	83		4 Guns 1st Pattern Wagons Br. 4 Wagons			5	10 1
8th Battery	4	141	44	83		4 Guns 8 Wagons			5	10 1
9th Battery	4	141	44	83		4 Guns 8 Wagons			5	10 1
Ammn. Column	4	167	34	143					29	125 1
TOTALS	21	643	194	299		12 guns 24 Wagons			48	160 5

RATION STRENGTH

To include Fighting Strength, Personnel detailed to march with the Train, and all Personnel and animals attached for Rations and Forage

Personnel Total, all Ranks entitled to Rations.	Horses and Mules		Other Animals	Mechanically Propelled Vehicles					Remarks
	Heavy Horses (14)	Other Horses and Mules (15)	(16)	Motor Cars (17)	Motor Bicycles (18) (19)	Lorries 3 Ton (20)	30 Cwt. (21)	Tractors (22)	(23)
58		35							1 4th Water Cart / 1 Cook house X
145		121							1 Maltese Cart
145		121							1 Telephone Cart
145		121							12 Gun Am. Gr. Wagons
171		177							do
									6 Std.
									1 Technical Stores
									1 Stot Timbered Wagons
									12 Wagons from Acc. for Compositions
664		535							48 Vehicles

Ammunition with Unit :—
·303 inch ; approximate number of rounds per Man _____
·303 inch ; " " " per Machine Gun _____
Gun or Howitzer ; approximate number of rounds per Gun or Howitzer _____

Supplies with Unit :—
Approximate number of days' rations for men of ration strength _____
" " " forage for Animals _____
" " " fuel and lubricants for Mechanically Propelled Vehicles _____

Signature of Commander _____ LIEUT. COLONEL
COMMANDING 1/3rd LONDON BRIGADE R.F.A.

Army Form B 231.

FIELD STATE.

To be rendered in accordance with Field Service Regulations, Part II.

Unit: 118th London Brigade R.F.A.
Place: Bordon, Hants.
Date: 27 Sept. 1915.

UNIT (1)	FIGHTING STRENGTH — Personnel			Horses and Mules		Other Animals (6)	Guns and Ammunition Wagons (stating nature) (8)	Machine Guns (9)	Ambulances (10)	Tool Carts, Technical Carts (stating nature) (11)	Remarks		RATION STRENGTH — Personnel	Horses and Mules		Other Animals (16)	Mechanically Propelled Vehicles		Lorries		Tractors (22)	Remarks (23)
	Officers (2)	Other Ranks (3)		Riding (4)	Draught and Pack (5)						Rifles	(12) Bicycles	Total all Ranks entitled to Rations (13)	Heavy Horses (14)	Other Horses and Mules (15)		Motor Cars (18)	Motor Bicycles (19)	3 Ton (20)	30 Cwt. (21)		
Headquarter Staff	3	37		28	7		Guns 18 pr Q.F. Personnel Wagons 18pr Q.F.			x		1	58		35							4 Water Carts
do. attd. A.V.C.	1	12																					4 G.S. Cart
do attd A.S.C. / R.A.M.C.	1	4																					
117th Battery	4	141		44	83		4 Guns 8 Wagons			4	5	1	145		127							1 Maltese Cart
118th Battery	4	141		44	83		4 Guns 8 Wagons			5	10	1	145		127							1 Telephone Cart
119th Battery	4	141		44	83		4 Guns 8 Wagons			5	10	1	145		127							12 Gun Am. G.S. Wagon
Ammun. Column	4	167		34	143					29	125	1	171		171							6 S.A.A. do. 1 Technical Store 7 S.A.A. Limbered Wagons
TOTALS	21	643		194	399		12 Guns 24 Wagons		x	48	160	5	664		593							12 Wagons from A.16. for Baggage & Forage 48 Vehicles

Ammunition with Unit:—
.303 inch; approximate number of rounds per Man _____
.303 inch; " " " " per Machine Gun _____
Gun or Howitzer; approximate number of rounds per Gun or Howitzer _____

Supplies with Unit:—
Approximate number of days' rations for men of ration strength _____
" " " " " forage for Animals _____
" " " " " fuel and lubricants for Mechanically Propelled Vehicles _____

Signature of Commander _____ LIEUT. COLONEL
COMMANDING 118th LONDON BRIGADE R.F.A.

Forms B 231 / 3

(79269.) Wt.W. 5870—621. 900,000 10/14. J. P. & Co. Ltd.

Army Form B 231.

FIELD STATE.

Unit _____
Place _____
Date _____

To be rendered in accordance with Field Service Regulations, Part II.

UNIT	FIGHTING STRENGTH - This should not include details attached to unit, or personnel detailed to march with the Train, or any men unit to go into action with unit											RATION STRENGTH - To include Fighting Strength, Personnel detailed to march with the Train, and all Personnel and animals attached for Rations and Forage										Remarks
	Personnel		Horses and Mules		Other Animals	Guns and Ammunition Wagons (stating nature)	Machine Guns	Ambulances	Tool Carts, Technical Carts (stating nature)	Remarks	Personnel	Horses and Mules		Other Animals	Motor Cars	Motor Bicycles	Lorries		Tractors	
	Officers	Other Ranks	Riding	Draught and Pack							Total, all Ranks entitled to Rations.	Heavy Horses	Other Horses and Mules				3 Ton	30 Cwt.		
(1)	(2)	(3)	(4)	(5)	(6)	(7)	(8)	(9)	(10)	(11)	(12)	(13)	(14)	(15)	(16)	(17)	(18)	(19)	(20)	(21)	(22)	(23)
TOTALS																						

Ammunition with Unit:—
.303 inch ; approximate number of rounds per Man _____
.303 inch ; " " " " per Machine Gun _____
Gun or Howitzer ; approximate number of rounds per Gun or Howitzer _____

Supplies with Unit:—
Approximate number of days' rations for men of ration strength _____
" " " " forage for Animals _____
" " " " fuel and lubricants for Mechanically Propelled Vehicles _____

Signature of Commander _____

(T9263.) Wt.W. 5870—621. 200,000 10/14. J. P. & Co. Ltd. Forms B 231 / 3

D/
74 37

36th Division

1/4th London Bde: R.F.A.

Vol I

Oct 15
/
Dec 15

CONFIDENTIAL

War Diary

of

1/4 London (How) Bde. R.F.A.?

from Oct. 1. 1915 to Oct. 31. 1915

Volume I.

Army Form C.2

WAR DIARY
or
INTELLIGENCE SUMMARY

1/4 London Howitzer Brigade R.F.A.

October 1915

(Erase heading not required.)

Instructions regarding War Diaries and Intelligence Summaries are contained in F.S. Regs., Part II. and the Staff Manual respectively. Title Pages will be prepared in manuscript.

Place	Date	Hour	Summary of Events and Information	Remarks and references to Appendices
BORDON	1/10/15		Completion re-equipment of Brigade	
	3/10/15	12.5 am	Left BORDON for SOUTHAMPTON	
			Embarked at SOUTHAMPTON	
		5.0 pm	Sailed	
HAVRE	4/10	4.50 am	arrived HAVRE	
			Rest camp	
	5/10	10.30 am	Left HAVRE by train	
		8.45 pm	arrived AMIENS	
VAUX-EN-AMIENOIE	6/10	2 am	arrived VAUX-EN-AMIENOIE	
	7/10		Exercise - ho nature a jnage	
	8/10		exercise	
	9/10		Drill ordr - Fired 1000 rounds H.E.	
	10/10		Fired 500 rounds H.E.	
	11/10		Drill ordr. Fired 500 rounds H.E.	
			tactics by C.R.A.	

Army Form C. 2118

WAR DIARY
or
INTELLIGENCE SUMMARY

1/4 London Howitzer Brigade

October 1915

Place	Date	Hour	Summary of Events and Information	Remarks and references to Appendices
VAUX-EN-AMIENOIS	12/10		In billets.	
	13/10		Inspection of billets by C.R.A. Bull oxen	
	14/10		Lt.Col. LEA leaves for ENGLAND. Major WAINWRIGHT assumes command	
	15/10		Battery parades	
	16/10		A General Field day	
	17/10		Divine service in Chateau grounds.	
	18/10		Battery parades	
			Captain DYMOTT to h.q/o.s.	
			Lieut MOREING Temporarily to A.C.	
			Lieut LAST Temporarily to 1/10 Battery	
	19/10		En repos hours	
			Brigade & Battery staff tours.	
	20/10		Party of firing batteries into action at or about MAILLY-MAILLET.	
			Brigade attached for instruction to 127 Bde R.F.A.	
MAILLY	22/10		Day spent by batteries taking over & laying telephone wires	

Army Form C. 2118

WAR DIARY
or
INTELLIGENCE SUMMARY

(Erase heading not required.)

1/4 London Howitzer Brigade R.F.A.

October 1915.

Place	Date	Hour	Summary of Events and Information	Remarks and references to Appendices
MAILLY	1915 23/10	11 am	1/11 Battery registered point K.30.c.85	Maps Reference: Trench maps 57D.N.E Sheet 3 & 4 part 9 57D.S.E Sheet 1 & 2 part 8
		2.30 pm	" " " K.30.c.7.7	
		3 pm	B.57 " German trenches at N.E. end of BEAUMONT–HAMEL	
		3.30 pm	C.57 " " " (Q.5.c.4.8)	
	24/10	noon	C.57 " " " Q.5.c.3.9	
	25/10		" " never at point Q.5.d.9.3	
			very wet. no shooting.	
	26/10	10.30 am	1/11 Battery registered K.30.c.56	
		10.45 "	" " K.29.D.9.7. (haystack)	
		noon	" " K.36. C.2.1. (enemy trench)	
		11 am	C.57 " " Q.5.B.9.5. communication trench	
		11.15 "	" " Q.5.d.6.2. dug out	
		11.30 "	" " Q.11.B.6.8. enemy trench	
		3.30 pm	1/10 " K.30.e.6.5. right hand corner of SERRE – communication trench	
		3 pm	B.57 " R.7.e.3.6. enemy redoubt.	
		3.30 "	" " R.7.a.1.3.	
		4 pm	" " Q.13.b.7.6 Station at BEAUCOURT–SUR–ANCRE	
	27/10	11.30 "	C.57 " Q.11.B.6.8. enemy trench	
		noon	" " Q.5.B.9.5. communication trench	

Army Form C. 2118

WAR DIARY
or
INTELLIGENCE SUMMARY
(Erase heading not required.)

1/4 London Howitzer Brigade R.F.A.

October 1915.

Instructions regarding War Diaries and Intelligence Summaries are contained in F. S. Regs., Part II. and the Staff Manual respectively. Title Pages will be prepared in manuscript.

Place	Date	Hour	Summary of Events and Information	Remarks and references to Appendices
MAILLY	27/10	3 p.m.	B.57 Batty. Registration Station build near BEAUCOURT-SUR-ANCRE (R.7.c.40) Registered 4 direct hits with lyddite when dust ht?	
		3.45	B.57 Batty. Registered Target (R.13.d.6.3)	
		4.15	B.57 " " (R.19.a.8.2)	
		3.45	1/10 " " (K.29.c.9.67)	
		4.20	1/10 " " (K.29.b.5.1)	
		3.0	1/10 " " (K.29.b.5.7)	
		3.30	1/10 " " (K.29.b.9.8)	
	28/10		Lt. Jagger organised 1/10 Batty.	
		12 noon	C/57 Batty. Registered Target (Q5.b.9.57)	
		11.30	1/10 " " (K.29.b.4.2)	
		11.25	1/10 " " (K.29.b.7.8)	
	29/10	12 noon	1/10 Registered Road & dug out (K.30.c.8.5)	
			1/10 " " house. (K.30.d.1.9)	
	30/10	10.45	1/10 " " (K.30.c.7.57)	
			Battery closed up position & got a telephone on site.	
BONNEVILLE	31/10		Men of [?] intercom trade to billeting area at BONNEVILLE	

A. Wauringh Major
LIEUT.-COL. R.F.A.
COMMANDING 1/4th LONDON HOWITZER BRIGADE

Army Form C. 2118

WAR DIARY
INTELLIGENCE SUMMARY
(Erase heading not required.)

Instructions regarding War Diaries and Intelligence Summaries are contained in F.S. Regs., Part II. and the Staff Manual respectively. Title Pages will be prepared in manuscript.

Place	Date	Hour	Summary of Events and Information	Remarks and references to Appendices
HAVRE	3/10/15		Travelled from BORDON to HAVRE, via SOUTHAMPTON. Transport S.S. COURTFIELD a cattle boat which provided excellent accommodation for horses.	
"	4/10/15		Quiet.	
"	5/10/15		Proceeded to AMIENS. via ROUEN. By train. Found cattle trucks very good for horse transport. Arrived at AMIENS 7.30 P.M & takes to VAUX.	
VAUX.	6/10/15		All horses except officers chargers picketed out. Horses not healthy, but then the ration of 12 lbs & 12 lbs. hay is insufficient for men of our so called "light draught" it is difficult to fatten them without extra forage. Horses 1/4 London RFA. & 1/4 London RFA. an gun, Vety charge of 109th Inf Bde, 150th Co. R.E. 30th Section Div Sup Col. & 109th Field Ambulance.	
"	7-10/10/15		Quiet.	
"	11/10/15		Gave Vety charge of A.S.C. at Pring.	
"	12/10/15		Quiet.	
"	13/10/15		Med. WAINWRIGHT R.H.A. took over 1/4 London R.F.A. from Lt Col. L.F.A. who returned to England.	
"	14/10/15		A.D.V.S. inspected 1/4 London R.F.A. Horses.	
"	15/10/15		Quiet.	
"	16/10/15		Divisional Field Day. I remained all day at the Divisional Depot Horses with a farrier. But there were no casualties.	
"	17-19/10/15		Quiet.	

WAR DIARY
INTELLIGENCE SUMMARY
(Erase heading not required.)

Army Form C. 2118

Place	Date	Hour	Summary of Events and Information	Remarks and references to Appendices
VAUX.	20/10/15		Proceeded to MAILY-MAILLETT with 4th Lieut. R.B.A. who was attached to 127 (Hows) Bde. R.F.A. 4th Division. Horses picketed out at FORCEVILLE about 2 miles from front line trenches, in orchards, for route from hostile aircraft. These have been all kept in temporary shelters mostly. The Horses of the 4th Div. look very well & are well made brick floors.	
FORCEVILLE	21/10/15		Reported to Major Jackson A.D.V.S. 4th Div.	
	22/10/15		Our horses now only get 10 lbs of hay per day, as we are unable to buy the others 2 lbs locally & the R.S.C. cannot supply it.	
	23-27/10/15		Quiet.	
	28/10/15		A.D.V.S. 4th Division inspected our horses & thought them very thin.	
	29/10/15		Discussed Infantry officer about to shoot his charger because it had fallen down & broke its knees. He refused to think that the knee was the same as broken leg. Rescued horse & sent it to Mobile Vety Section. Think that before by officers who are allowed charges should be taught something about them.	
	30/10/15		Quiet.	
	31/10/15		Brigade moved to Bonneville (BONNEVILLE). Horses again picketed out. During the month the Horses have been very free from disease. The only contagious skin disease was a few cases of ringworm & there was no infectious disease. The Lines were now afflicted a little better & in better condition.	

36 ct
6 38 ct 13.12.15

1/4 London Scot. R.F.A.
Nov
Vol II

CONFIDENTIAL.

War Diary

of

1/4th London (How) Bde. R.F.A.T.

from Nov 1. 1915 to Nov. 30. 1915

Volume I

[signature]
Lt. Col. Comdg
1/4 London F. A. Bde.

Army Form C. 2118

1/4 kinres ?.?.Q. ?.

WAR DIARY
or
INTELLIGENCE SUMMARY

(Erase heading not required.)

Instructions regarding War Diaries and Intelligence Summaries are contained in F. S. Regs., Part II. and the Staff Manual respectively. Title Pages will be prepared in manuscript.

Place	Date	Hour	Summary of Events and Information	Remarks and references to Appendices
BONNEVILLE	Nov. 1		Quiet day	
	2		Inspection of billets by C.O.	
	3		Shell order. Battery arrangements.	
	4		Lieut A.H. horning left sick -	
	5		Quiet day - exercise.	
	6		a Divisional Artillery Tactical Exercise -	
			Quiet day - Battery arrangements.	
	7		Lieut Bowater joined & was posted to 1/10 Battery - Regimental Bath house started -	Lt BOWATER
	8		Divine Service. C.J.E. 11.4.45. Battle. 9 am. hivergement 3 pm	
	9		B.57 & C.57 batteries received orders to be ready for embarkation - MARSEILLES -	
	10		Inspection of horses by C.R.A.	
	11		Quiet day	
	12		D.D.R 3rd army & A.V.C. Inspected inoculated horses. Inspection of 1/10 Battery by C.O.	
	13		Inspection of 1/11 Battery by C.O.	
	14		Battery arrangements.	
	15		Reconnoitred for divisional artillery Tactical exercise.	
			Divisional Artillery tactical exercise. B. Battery gun 100 rounder at troops horses work -	
			Ships BEAUVAL	
	16		64 Remounts arrive from Horse Int. section.	
	17		2Lt E.R. BARTLETT - joined & was posted to 1/11 Battery for instruction -	
			Reconnaissance by fn Brigade -	
			Brigade tactical in coast.	
	18		B.57 & C.57 batteries & a hq for ammunition columns left at 10 pm. to entrain for Port of embarkation	

1875 Wt. W593/826 1,000,000 4/15 J.B.C. & A. A.D.S.S./Forms/C. 2118.

WAR DIARY or INTELLIGENCE SUMMARY

Army Form C. 2118

Place	Date	Hour	Summary of Events and Information	Remarks and references to Appendices
BONNEVILLE	Nov. 19		Field General Court Martial held at Headquarters 1/10 Battery given for ordeal to the Heavy Howitz Workshops BEAUVAL.	
	20		Battery arrangements. 2 Lt. EDGSON arrived & was attached for instruction to the 1/10 Battery.	
	21		XIII Corps took over administration & command of 36th DIVISION. Church Parades.	
	22		Inspection of Ammunition Column & Headquarters staff by C.O.	
	23		Orders received for movement of 1/10 & 1/11 Batteries & Ammunition Col. into action – Movement of 1/10 Battery & Section B Am. Col. & proportional part of D.A.C. to 7th Corps area to join 48th Division at THIEVRES –	
	24		Movement of 1/11 Battery & Section A Am. Col. & proportional part of D.A.C. to 10th Corps area to join 51st Division at WARLOY-BAILLON.	
	25		Brigade Headquarters to remain at BONNEVILLE. Funds now for Brigade Staff. REVD. NOBLETTS to transferred to 1/2 LONDON BDE. No. 3 Section 36th Div. Am. Col. arrived from BERNAVILLE & to be under Lt. Col. WAINEWRIGHT	
	26		Orders received for move to new divisional billeting area.	
	27		Advance party gone to LES MASURES to fix billets	
	28		Movement of Headquarters staff into new billets at LES MASURES –	
	29		Quiet day	
	30		Field Service training under Brigade staff	

Army Form C. 2118

WAR DIARY
INTELLIGENCE SUMMARY
(Erase heading not required.)

Instructions regarding War Diaries and Intelligence Summaries are contained in F.S. Regs., Part II. and the Staff Manual respectively. Title Pages will be prepared in manuscript.

Place	Date	Hour	Summary of Events and Information	Remarks and references to Appendices
BONNEVILLE	1-2/11/15		Quiet.	
"	3/11/15		A.D.V.S. inspected horses. Watering arrangements very poor, but the Brigade has built troughs which have to be filled by buckets as we are not allowed a pump. Once a day the horses are watered at Trieffles. Gave Vety. Charge of 109th Infantry Bde.	
"	4-5/11/15		Quiet. Gave Vety. Charge of 109th Field Ambulance & 109th Infantry.	
"	6/11/15		Gave Vety. Charge of 30th Div. Train A.S.C. The horses of the 1/4th London R.F.A. Their horses are in very poor condition.	
"	7-10/11/15		Quiet. The horses of the 1/4th London R.F.A. are put under cover.	
"	11/15		The D.R.O. A.D.V.S. condemned cast 13 of the horses of the 1/4th Ldn. R.F.A. & several more will be transferred to other units. 9th Batt. R. Innis. Fus. sent 27 horses to Mobile Vety Sect. suffering from debility. Another due to standing in mud on horse lines on frosty nights.	
"	12/11/12		All the horses of 9th Batt R. Innis. Fus. were put under cover. Discovered rough attempt the horses of the inhabitants of Bonneville (BONNEVILLE) & that every precaution I could it spreading to our own horses.	
"	13-15/11/12		Quiet.	
"	16/15		1/4 Ldn. R.F.A. got 52 Remts to which came out by train to Rail Head at DOULLENS & were distributed from the 48th Mobile Vety Sect. A very good start of horses.	
"	17/15		Quiet.	
"	18/15		B & C Batteries & ½ Ammunit. Col. 1/4th Ldn. R.F.A. proceeded to MARSELLES via AMIENS.	
"	19/11/15 20-22/11/15		Quiet.	

Army Form C. 2118

WAR DIARY
INTELLIGENCE SUMMARY
(Erase heading not required.)

Instructions regarding War Diaries and Intelligence Summaries are contained in F. S. Regs., Part II. and the Staff Manual respectively. Title Pages will be prepared in manuscript.

Place	Date	Hour	Summary of Events and Information	Remarks and references to Appendices
BONNEVILLE	23/15		10th & 11th Batteries & advancing Bdys of Ammn Col. set out to the Fd. Headquarters Staff 1/4 Lnd. RDA arrived behind.	
"	24-27/15		Quiet.	
"	28/15		Headq'rs 1/4th Ldn. RDA moved to LES MASURES 10 miles E. of ABBEVILLE. Horses sick & cattle.	
LES MASURES	29/15		Quiet.	
"	30/15		Pet. - Vety. Charge of 102nd Inf. Bde., 121st Co. R.E., Bn. I.C. O.S.C.	

56 DIV
ATTACHED 38 DIV

2352

Headquarters
London Artillery
Attached 38th Welsh Division.

[Stamp: 1/4TH LONDON HOWITZER BRIGADE No. M.D. 640 Date 31.12.15]

CONFIDENTIAL.

War Diary
of
1/4 LONDON HOWITZER BRIGADE. R.F.A.

from December 1st. 1915 to Dec. 31st. 1915

Volume 1.

2352

A.D. Wainwright Lt. Col.
1/4 London Howitzer Brigade R.F.A.

1/4 London Bde R.F.A.
Dec. Vol II A.
Drawn 36th (to Diam. Corr. Div. 3.1.16.)

From 36th 13.12.15

Army Form C. 2118

1/4 London. Howitzer Brigade. R.F.A.

WAR DIARY
or
INTELLIGENCE SUMMARY
(Erase heading not required.)

Instructions regarding War Diaries and Intelligence Summaries are contained in F.S. Regs., Part II. and the Staff Manual respectively. Title Pages will be prepared in manuscript.

Place	Date	Hour	Summary of Events and Information	Remarks and references to Appendices
LES MASURES	1/12/15		Quiet day.	
	2/12/15		Still active.	
	3/12/15		Exercises.	
	4/12/15		Drill order.	Lt. Col. WAINEWRIGHT goes on leave.
	5/12/15		Exercises.	
	6/12/15		Exercises.	1/0 & 1/11 Batteries & Am. Col. return from firing line - learnt that Brigade will shortly move to the 1st Army.
	7/12/15		Still active.	
	8/12/15		Battery arrangements.	
	9/12/15		Exercise.	
	10/12/15			
	11/12/15		Antiaircraft Exer. to 1/4m 173rd Bde. R.F.A.	
	12/12/15	2 pm	Brigade turns LES MASURES. Bivouacs at PONT REMY	
PONT REMY		3 pm	Brigade entrains. rais over 7 hours late.	
PECQUEUR	13/12/15	7.30 am	detrain at THIENNES & arrive into billets at PECQUEUR. Is attached to 38th WELSH Division. XI Corps. 1st Army. W/E Battery & Am Col billets at NEUF PRÉ.
	14/12/15		Quiet day. Lt. Col. WAINEWRIGHT returns from leave.	
	15/12/15		Exercise. Battery arrangements.	
	16/12/15		- do -	
	17/12/15			
	18/12/15		orders to be ready to move to region of HAVERSKERQUE.	
PECQUEUR - CORBIE	19/12/15		Hdqrs. into new billets at CORBIE 5 Kilo. W. J MERVILLE.	
CORBIE	20/12/15		Clearing up new billets. Battery arrangements.	
	21/12/15		" " Recve orders to move to new billets area. W. J AIRE.	
	22/12/15			
	23/12/15			
CORBIE - GLOMENGHEM	24/12/15		March to new billets at GLOMENGHEM.	
GLOMENGHEM	25/12/15		CHRISTMAS DAY. Kept as far as possible as a holiday.	
	26/12/15		Exercises. Lt. N.V. BOWATER evacuated to Base sick.	
	27/12/15		Still active.	
	28/12/15		Battery arrangements.	
	29/12/15		Trooper Larned that Brigade is about to move to join another Division. No 663 Bdr. Marshall C.J. 1/11 Battery tried by C.O. for F.G.C.M.
	30/12/15			
	31/12/15		Quiet day.	

A. Wainewright Lt. Col.
1/4 London Howitzer Brigade. R.A.

DISMOUNTED CAVALRY DIVISION

56 DIV

DIVISIONAL ARTY

1-4TH LONDON HOWITZER BDE R.F.A.

JAN - FEB 1916

B.M. C/52.

Dismounted Division.

        Herewith War Diary for month of January, 1916.
for   H.Q. Dismounted Divisional Artillery.
        1/4th London Brigade R.F.A. (How.)

Re your D.G. 44.

H.Q. Artillery,   Bde. Major,
Dismounted Division.   Dismounted Division Artillery.

1/2/16

WAR DIARY or INTELLIGENCE SUMMARY

Army Form C. 2118

1/4 London Howitzer Brigade R.F.A.

(Erase heading not required.)

Place	Date	Hour	Summary of Events and Information	Remarks and references to Appendices
CUINCHEM(?)	1 Jan		2/Lt. R.S. NASH posted as adjutant. Notified that The Brigade will have to join the 1st. Corps. Howitzer Section of 10 D.A.C. to be attached to the Brigade.	Map Reference Series B. 1/20,000
	2 Jan 3 Jan 4 Jan 5 Jan		Quiet day. Notified we are going to join Dismounted Cavalry Division. C.R.A. Dismounted cavalry Division calls to see C.O. Brigade Representative go to NOEULLES to see positions to be taken over from 8th London Brigade R.F.A.	Sheet No. 36 C.N.W.
NOEULLES LES VERMELLES	6 Jan	6 p.m.	1 Section of 1/10 Battery goes into action at A.25.D.30. 1 Section of 1/11 Battery goes in action at C.14.D.46.	Sheet No. 36 B.N.E.
	7 Jan	6 p.m. 6 p.m.	Headquarters at L.11.C.65. Wagon lines at BAILLY LABOURSE F.27.C.6.3. Ammn. col. & section D.A.C. go into billets at E.3.C.10.3. ANNEZIN Other two sections of battalion arrive in their positions. 1/10 registers guns C.S. H.6.2. Enclosure for G.12.13.0.8 inclusive. from G.4.A.9.0 to BULL'S BLUFF G.5.A.6.2.	Trench Map 36 C.N.W. Sheet 1&3
?	8 Jan	10.50 am 2.30 9 pm 9 pm 8.15	10 rounds retaliation. Opened onto C.7.5. SLAG ALLEY. Registered - G.37.A.107. 4 Shells LITTLE WILLIE. Supporting call by 1/11 battery. 15 rounds fired in SLAG ALLEY G.S.A.107 (1/11 Battery Both batteries registered. 3 shells in CITE ST ELIE in retaliation.	
	Jan. 10.		First very quiet. Sq. Sergt. F.O.O. Report machine gun replacement in O.P. on S.W. face of Hohen. Crater at HAIRPIN A few shells on our trenches about 7mm. 10-10.30 am 1/10 Bty registered Fosse Alley with 25 rounds.	10-11 am 1/10 Retaliate Can Rd HAISNES 16 Rounds. 12.30 am "Registers LITTLE WILLIE (54.B) 5 Rounds.
		10.10 am 2 pm	engaged enemy working party A.6.C.0.3. 6 Rounds. registers Cam Rd. HAISNES with 18 Rounds.	
		11.25 - 11.50 12 - 3.0 pm	Sq. Sergt. Rabbitt to Earl. Hosed St Elie. Repeat took in St Elie and HAISNES with 40 Rounds.	

Army Form C. 2118

WAR DIARY
or
INTELLIGENCE SUMMARY
1/4TH LONDON HOWITZER BRIGADE.

(Erase heading not required.)

Instructions regarding War Diaries and Intelligence Summaries are contained in F.S. Regs, Part II. and the Staff Manual respectively. Title Pages will be prepared in manuscript.

Place	Date	Hour	Summary of Events and Information	Remarks and references to Appendices
VERMELLES.	JAN. 11.		Front fairly quiet. 2 Enemy Aeroplanes were observed flying S.E. during the morning. It is reported that 2 North Lorries were destroyed by shell fire in ANNEQUIN. ENEMY. The shelled the following places during the morning with H.E. shells. ANNEQUIN, CAMBRIN, PUITS 13, Trenches near HOHENZOLLERN REDOUBT.	
		10 am – 2 pm	1/10 Retaliated on ST ELIE, and on CRATER. G.12.d.4.6. – Allequin 61 Puits. 1/11 Registered {S.9.B. A.28.B.4.1.} 43 Rounds Allequin. {A.30.B.4.8.}	
		7.25 pm	54½ Siège L. Section Redoubt HAISNES. A.30.B.S.E. with 10 Rounds.	
		12.10 pm	" Registered Corons. A.30.C. with 10 Rounds.	
		2.50 pm	" " " " 9 "	
			" S.E. corner of Europe.	
	JAN. 12.	10.15 am	2 German Aeroplanes were observed. At 10.30. 4 German observation balloons observed. Enemy working party observed at Q.5.B.6.8. This target was accurately engaged by 1/10 Battery. The enemy shelled our trenches intermittingly from 11.30. & 2.15 pm. At 1.30 pm 10, 8" shells fell just west of FOSSE. 9. in ANNEQUIN.	
		11.50 am	1/10 Registered points on trenches. 15 Rounds.	
		12.25 pm	Enemy working party. Q.5.B.6.8. 4 Rounds.	
		1.30	Registered CRATER. Q.12.d.4.6. and retaliated on same 15 Rounds.	
		12 – 1 pm	1/11 Registered CORONS ALLEY {A.28.D.9.0.} 15 Rounds {A.29.A.2.11}	
		"	" CITÉ ST ELIE H.1.C.5.4. 15 Rounds.	

WAR DIARY or INTELLIGENCE SUMMARY

Army Form C. 2118

1/4TH LONDON HOWITZER BRIGADE.

(Erase heading not required.)

Instructions regarding War Diaries and Intelligence Summaries are contained in F.S. Regs., Part II. and the Staff Manual respectively. Title Pages will be prepared in manuscript.

Place	Date	Hour	Summary of Events and Information	Remarks and references to Appendices
NOYELLES LES VERMELLES	Jan 13	10 am-12 nn	Left of 26 mm from Pont. arrived on the 12th posted to Batteries & Ammn Col on the 13th inst. 1/10 Battery retaliated with 50 rounds on Trench on their immediate front. Registered communication trench with 6 rounds	
		12.30 pm	1/4 Battery registered 18 " M.G. Emplacement. Retaliation on front trench with 8 rounds.	
		1.30 pm	Left section 59th Siege Registered – "The Coron" 6 rounds – "The Dump" 6 rounds. Point on Tenable 14 Rounds. No 4 Gun 1/10 Battery out of action. Inspected by I.O.M. Brigade Artificer to return soon	
	Jan 14		Front very quiet. Weather wild and fine.	
		11am-2pm	1/10 Battery Observation fair. 7 Horses removed to mobile action from S.A.C. Forage inspected.	
		3.25 pm	59th Siege Left Section. 15 rounds checking Rain trench registration. Retaliated 24 rounds on trench. (3.50 pm)	
		8.55 am	1/10 Battery Retaliation 13 Rnds on May Alley. 5.30 pm Large quantity of smoke seen rising from enemy trenches. G.C.C. 2½.8. (1:10000 MAP 36c NW 3)	
			No 4 Gun 1/10 Battery out of action	
	Jan 15	11.10 am	1/10 Battery Registered with 18 rounds Trenches S.E of Dump. Day very quiet. No 4 Gun 1/10 Battery out of action	
	Jan 16	10-12 nn	1/10 Battery Registration of Slag Alley 24 Rounds. No 4 Gun 1/10 Battery out of action	
		12.30 pm	1/10 " " " on CRATER. 20 Rounds	
		12.15 pm	1/4 " Retaliation on SLAG ALLEY. 8 Rounds During the day O.C. Brigade reconnoitred alternative gun positions. Day fairly quiet.	
	Jan 17		Fine and dry. Observation fairly good. 7mm and 1 officer went on Leave.	
		12.25 pm 1.55 pm	1/10 Battery shot 84 Rounds on MOUNDS on CRATER. Much damage was done, and granduses of timber on fire. The trench (Forward) was cleared and the Wanklis R.N.A cooperated.	
		11.15 am 2.30 pm	1/4 " Registered Harvin Village 20 Rounds. Also 23 rounds registering Points on trenches.	
		12.10 pm	59th Siege Left Section Retaliated on HAISNES. 3 North Buttons Points and 2 enemy aeroplanes patrolled from 10 am to 12 noon	
	Jan 18		Day was fair. Front quiet at 7.32 and 10.25 am the enemy shelled VERMELLES during the day the enemy shelled on trenches with 4.2 shells. We retaliated at different times during the day firing altogether 25 rounds.	
	Jan 19	10-12	Enemy Aeroplane (2) patrolled in front they were engaged by our A.A aircraft guns without success 2.45 Paint . Sniper were very active. We fired 33 rounds into HAISNES in Retaliation in fire on our trenches. At 4.30 the enemy shelled trenchpoints with heavy shell (4 inch, 6")	

1/4TH LONDON HOWITZER BRIGADE.

Army Form C. 2118

WAR DIARY or INTELLIGENCE SUMMARY

(Erase heading not required.)

Instructions regarding War Diaries and Intelligence Summaries are contained in F.S. Regs, Part II. and the Staff Manual respectively. Title Pages will be prepared in manuscript.

Place	Date	Hour	Summary of Events and Information	Remarks and references to Appendices
VERMELLES	JAN. 20	11 – 12.30	1/10 Battery Retaliated with 9 Rounds on HAISNES and 6 Rounds on POTSDAM TRENCH	Hostile Aeroplane observed patrolling N & E between 11.30 and 12. Last seen flying in direction of Mellust. On the whole were staying quiet.
		1.15	" " " 4 " " SLAG ALLEY	
		10.30–12	" " " 38 " " WATER TOWER A.29.C	
		1.10	" " " 6 " " SLAG ALLEY	
		2 pm	" " " 20 " " " "	
		2.15	" " " 9 " " LITTLE WILLIE	
		2.30	" " " 22 " " CENTRE OF DUMP G.5.A. and registration	
		3.15	The enemy shelled our support trenches at intervals during the day	
	JAN 21		1/4 Repulsed right hand side of Dump with 16 rounds at 4pm. Retaliated on Cité St Elie with 15 rounds at 4.15pm	
		11.30–3	Retaliated on Potsdam Trench and SLAG ALLEY 24 Rds	
		3.15	1/10 Registrat point on Trenches with 38 rounds. During the morning enemy shelled Inugeau & Morochville	
		8.30–11	S.9 also FOSSE E.3. In the afternoon they shelled WATER TOWER VERMELLES AND FOSSE 3 with A.2 and S.9. The day was quiet, nothing to report	
	JAN. 23		Hostile aeroplanes patrolled our front from 11.30 to 2.10 pm. 10th and 11th Battery front 42 Rounds allyette shell Repetition and registers some new points in the trench. The day was clear. Enemy shelled our trenches slightly and fired heavily for what there was on the Battrie of Vermelles	
	JAN. 22		During the morning they fired 里 (4's) HE (4's) about 9.24 and at 2 pm 78 HE (4.2) in various places. Vermelles who also shelled about 5.9. (4's) at 2.30 on Rly crossing G.14.C	
			A civilian was seen taken notes of our Empire Aeroplane news from 9 that had come across. He was handed over to the M.P. Two white Rocket were observed 11.5 am leaving from G.7.B.8.VI. leading 100 Five. He retaliated on front line several times during the day.	
	JAN. 24		Very very quiet. At 3.15 pm an officer took place in sight of our Lines. No information available. R shell struck 10th Battery OP.(Westmouth) slight damage Caubrain also Water Tower, A.26.C.9%.4. and Water Tower G.8, D.5, 6.	
		3–4 pm	The 11th Battery Retaliation with 16 Rnd. on HAISNES and St ELIE	

WAR DIARY or INTELLIGENCE SUMMARY

Army Form C. 2118

1/4th LONDON HOWITZER BRIGADE

(Erase heading not required.)

Instructions regarding War Diaries and Intelligence Summaries are contained in F.S. Regs., Part II. and the Staff Manual respectively. Title Pages will be prepared in manuscript.

Place	Date	Hour	Summary of Events and Information	Remarks and references to Appendices
VERMELLES	JAN 25	10–12 pm	The front was normal. From 8.40 to 2.55 pm enemy aeroplanes. Two bombs were dropped. Hostile observation balloon observed at 8.30 am. The enemy shelled Estorie, VERMELLES church, also Rly at G.14.C. WATER TOWER at A.26.C.4%.4.	
		10.57	11th Battery Ridiculed with 60 Rnds, on parts in trench and on HAISNES	
		3 pm	10th Battery Registered points on trench with 39 Rnds. Tested sight on new gun in place of No 4 condemned by I.O.M. with 5 Rounds	
	JAN.26	7–9 am	3 Observation balloons were sighted over the town from G.14.C.4½.6. Day was normal. Enemy still his marginal at 10.2 pm from 1/10 front 19 Brdicits ST ELIE and ½ front	
		1.10 pm	10th Bty Retaliates with 5 Rnds on enemy trenches. 20 Rnds into HAISNE, an aeroplane about arranged	
		12–2.0 pm	11th By Registed point on trench with 37 Rnds. by DIV Hapts	
	JAN. 27	8 am	Our observation balloon received range from our previous day. Enemy intermittently shelled our front line opposite G.14.C.4½.6.	
		3 pm	11th Bty with HE also 150 77mm on second line trench. A hostile Aeroplane over VERMELLES 3 at 1.30 pm	
		11 am	1/10th Retaliates 69 Rnds on Hostile TRENCHES [in passiveretion from By OPS]	
			1/11th " 12 " " " "	
		12.40 pm	59th Siege Bty Section Retaliates on Trenches with 4 Rounds	
		5 pm	do do HAISNES " 6 "	
	JAN. 28	10 am	Enemy opened intense bombardment of our trenches. The gas lights about 12.30 pm but received its intensity about 3.15 pm. Lasted about 5 pm. VERMELLES and PHILOSOPHE were also shelled. During the day 10th & 11th 4ty retaliated on enemy trench with about 250 Rnds 59th Siege fired 18 Rnds during morning on THE DUMP and COBONS in retaliation	
	JAN. 30		The front was normal. Haversian toil - morning very misty. The enemy shelled our trenche and also put a few shells into Phillips 10th and 11th Battery Retaliated on enemy trenches. In night shot about arranged by the R.A. Hqrs. took place, from 9 pm to 6.30 am in the 30th. Battery front in alter point in the trench the 10th front 60 Rnds – the 11th 63 –	

1875 Wt. W593/826 1,000,000 4/15 J.B.C. & A. A.D.S.S./Forms/C. 2118.

Army Form C. 2118

WAR DIARY
or
INTELLIGENCE SUMMARY

14th LONDON HOWITZER BRIGADE.

(Erase heading not required.)

Instructions regarding War Diaries and Intelligence Summaries are contained in F.S. Regs., Part II. and the Staff Manual respectively. Title Pages will be prepared in manuscript.

Place	Date	Hour	Summary of Events and Information	Remarks and references to Appendices
HERMELLES.	30 JAN.		The day was very misty. Observation almost impossible. The enemy shewn Phosphor bombs. The 11th Battery fired altogether 55 rnds in retaliation on the enemy trenches.	
	29/1/16		The 10th Retaliates with 20 on various point of Enemy trench.	
	4.12 pm		The 10th by order R.A H.Q.ts engaged hostile Trench Mortar G.12.a.3.6 and fired 40 Rounds.	
			In the evening 5.30 pm enemy fired 6 H.E into Phillosophe and at 8.0 pm 14 – H.E. in MAZINGARBE.	
	31 JAN.	11 am	Any fairly quiet. Observation difficult owing to mist.	
		11.30	1/10 Battery retaliates on Potsdam Trench. G.S.D.8.8. 24 Rounds	
		11.30 "	" TRENCH MORTAR. G.12. A.4.5. with 15 Rounds. Several direct hits reported.	
		11.45 "	Reported Sniper POST G.S.18.11½.8½ with 15 Rounds. O.P reported destroyed.	
		12.0 "	" SLAG ALLEY, G.S.A.9½.6½ with 10 Rounds	
		12.5 "	Retaliates with 50 Rounds SLAG ALLEY G.S.A.	
		From 9.0 to 12.15	The enemy shelled MOROC, VERMELLES and trenches about G.15.A altogether about 70 shell, all 4.2.	

alkamming[?]
LIEUT.-COL. R.F.A.
COMMANDING 14th LONDON HOWITZER BRIGADE.

56

Appendix to
War Diary Vol IV

1/4th London Hons. Bde. R.F.A.

WAR DIARY for
FEBRUARY, 1916.

Army Form C. 2118

WAR DIARY
INTELLIGENCE SUMMARY
(Erase heading not required.)

FEB. 1916
1/4th LONDON HOWITZER BRIGADE.

Instructions regarding War Diaries and Intelligence Summaries are contained in F.S. Regs., Part II. and the Staff Manual respectively. Title Pages will be prepared in manuscript.

Place	Date	Hour	Summary of Events and Information	Remarks and references to Appendices
VERMELLES	FEB 1		The front was normal and quiet. Front made observation difficult. Enemy aeroplanes observed patrolling our front during the morning. The enemy shelled our support trenches in NOYELLES. The 1/10 Battery fired altogether 12 rounds in retaliation during the day. A shoot was arranged by Divl. Arty. to take place on the 2nd of Feb. A draft of 7 men + A.B.O.s arrived from Havre. New maps arrived with orders to take same into use at 12 midnight 2/3 Feb.	
	2		The front was quiet. An enemy aeroplane was observed at 1 p.m. About 30 shell fell with PHILOSOPHE none being dropped also fell on our support trenches. The shoot arranged by Div Arty was carried out. It is reported this much damage was done and trenches and HQ material was thrown into the air. The 2nd section 59th Siege (6") co-operated. The targets in the report were machine gun emplacements by the HAIRPIN and by the CRATER. We withdrew a mine near the HAIRPIN at 8.45 p.m. This was afterwards unsuccessfully occupied by our troops. The 1/10th Battery cooled with slow fire.	
	3		Morning clear but high wind. Observation good. 3 Enemy Aeroplanes observed during the morning. Very little shelling. No 8.9 shrek opposite near that Battery. One casualty, slight concussion sent to field Hospital. A night shoot arranged by Divl. Arty HQrs. This was stopped at 11.25 p.m. by orders from Divl. Arty. HQ.	
	4		Front normal. A few shell into VERMELLES and in our trenches. Lt N.N. Bowater returned from leave to England - which left our strength. Enemy mine exploded to go off within next 48 hours - 10" Battery. given two points to fire on above the mine place.	
	5	3.45 2.30	The morning was quiet - observation good. 4 Enemy observation balloons observed. Some activity on part of enemy lines. Both near WINDOW and work observed to have been done on enemy trenches in TERRORS places. Two teams were observed morning from HAISNES towards DOUVRIN. 59th Siege and 1/4 Battery shot wild. Enemy aeroplane observation. At 10.45 and 12.20 Enemy Aeroplanes patrolled front. Enemy activity with trench mortar on ESSEX TRENCH was observed to fire from 1/11 L Battery. Enemy shelled our support trenches lightly, and put shorts to shell into 1st RUTOIRE and PHILOSOPHE. he retaliated on enemy trenches, also reported some bursts on trenches. 1/11 L Battery fired 8 rounds or trenches on night firing above by new Divl Arty Orders.	

Army Form C. 2118

WAR DIARY
or
INTELLIGENCE SUMMARY

(Erase heading not required.)

1/4TH LONDON HOWITZER BRIGADE.

Instructions regarding War Diaries and Intelligence Summaries are contained in F.S. Regs., Part II. and the Staff Manual respectively. Title Pages will be prepared in manuscript.

Place	Date	Hour	Summary of Events and Information	Remarks and references to Appendices
VERMELLES	FEB 6		The Front was quiet and normal. Observation fairly good. Enemy Artillery fairly active. About 70 H.2 shell on Rly line about G.14.D. About 12 on PHILOSOPHE. No retaliation on their trench during the day. The 59th Siege registered some points.	
	7.		The Front was quiet and normal. One enemy Aeroplane was observed over Vermelles 3.45 pm. About 70 H.2 shell fell in front of 11th Battery Position (A.27.C.) during the day. Also a few on MAZINGARBE and VERMELLES. A practice gas alarm was received at Bde Office at 7.53 am. the Battery all "stood to" at their battle stations until gas helmets adjusted. 10th + 11th fired some 2 rounds and 59th Siege fired one round. This was timed out altogether 4 minutes. 15 gas helmets were condemned and Hefft Stoff (Bde) received 30 new helmets from Amn Dep Kempt. The 10th Battery registered new hostile trenches with 32 Rounds. Also 1 Bty reported enemy hot shelled and destroyed one of our O.Ps. Asked no. 2 detachment on enemy O.P. line (11th Battery) retaliated with 50 rnds and saw enemy O.P. to pieces at (A.27.C.4.D.)	
	8		The front was quiet and normal. Day fairly good. No observation. 5 hostile observation balloons up. Enemy Aeroplanes patrolled front at 10 am and at 11.15am. Again at 3.20 pm. Enemy shell shelled in front of VERMELLES about 100 H.2 shell. Also on 4 from POSIE 9. A few shells on our support trenches. The 1/11 Battery retaliated on Enemy trenches. 59th Siege registered front on trenches 2 Bnds.	
	9		Front normal. Observation very good. 2 Observation balloons of Enemy observed. 4 Hostile planes sighted at 2 pm travelling NE & NW. 7 Planes over VERMELLES each approach to go towards BETHUNE and fractured to enemy line. Another Aeroplane was sighted at 2.35 pm. Very little both pm. - a few shells into VERMELLES - 1/10th & 1/11th Registered some anywhere enemy O.P.S. 59th Siege registered some front on the trenches. Enemy Bomd 33 And Bty everylate position with A view to taking our anti aircraft up.	

A.W. Browning Lt Col

WAR DIARY or INTELLIGENCE SUMMARY

Army Form C. 2118

1/4TH LONDON HOWITZER BRIGADE

(Erase heading not required.)

Instructions regarding War Diaries and Intelligence Summaries are contained in F.S. Regs., Part II. and the Staff Manual respectively. Title Pages will be prepared in manuscript.

Place	Date	Hour	Summary of Events and Information	Remarks and references to Appendices
	10		Morning fine observation fair. Front Normal. No hostile Aeroplanes or Balloons observed. A few small shell fell on our support trenches. We retaliated on enemy trenches and reported some occupied O.P's.	
	11		Front was normal. Rain and low light made observation difficult. Between 10-11.30am our trenches were shelled by enemy. We retaliated on hostile trenches. Col Harper + officer of 53 Brl Arty came to inspect positions that they were going to take over from us on the 13th. At 2.30 pm this move was cancelled and it was decided that the 58th would not relieve us.	
	11(Con)		About 4 pm there was some shelling by enemy on MR batteries + M.G activity on the part of the enemy. This gradually developed into a small bombardment of our support trenches. We retaliated. We retaliated with about 150 Rounds on enemy trenches fire ceased about 6pm. The 59th Siege who retaliated with ——— 8 rounds on HAISNES	
	12		This morning the enemy shelled our trenches and about 3pm a fairly heavy bombardment took place and first north of our Zone. finally ceased about 4pm. We retaliated about 440 Shells.	
	13		Considerable Artillery activity throughout the day chiefly on the northern part of the zone. 8 enemy Aeroplanes observed. About 11am it was reported that an Enemy Aeroplane troop dropped by our Anti aircraft became. Any fair observation good. Enemy fired about 500 shells at our support trenches. About 33% were Shrk. We retaliated on trenches with about 180. H.S Shells 18, 6" from 59th Siege. 10 fr/hr Battry A.162 covered battery came into position 6 pm in front right of 1/24 Position.	
	13(Con)		Between about 5.15 pm and 6 pm some bombs of enemy infantry reached our front trench under an curtain of heavy fire. Three Rockets were sent up. We were firing at the time and continued firing. See 1/24th Diary. About 100 men 1000 rounds our Battery fired on 100 rounds. The enemy who was not apparently got the trenches fire under control.	

1875 Wt. W593/826 1,000,000 4/15 J.B.C.&A. A.D.S.S./Forms/C.2118.

WAR DIARY or INTELLIGENCE SUMMARY

Army Form C. 2118

1/4TH LONDON HOWITZER BRIGADE.

(Erase heading not required.)

Place	Date	Hour	Summary of Events and Information	Remarks and references to Appendices
VERMELLES	FEB. 14		The front was normal. Barometer fair. High wind. Reported that enemy had forced up two of their own heads running out from P.1 line trench. Two aeroplanes observed. Enemy shelled our trench during the day but not heavily.	
	15		Front normal, Barometer fair. High wind. Day very quiet. No return on part of enemy artillery. We did not fire all day.	
	16.		Front normal. Barometer fell but High. Wind. The footpath showing at the Aintillery at Annerie was struck by 2 shells. We fired 24 rounds.	
	17.		The front was normal and fairly quiet. From 9.45 a.m. to 10.15 a.m. the road from Boyelles to Sailly to Berres was shelled with single shells every 100 yards. These shells appeared to be T.S.G. The enemy shelled our support trench generally with 77 m and 5.9. Two shells about 1.15 pm burst H.E. from Germans was heard using an O.P. in turret. J.5.B.1.5. Two target was enrift near 6 shells fired on it. An observed shoot was commenced by April Artillery in corporation with the howitz from 1 pm to 2.30. The 102nd Battery fired 123 rounds and the 112th 80 rounds. Two short was reported to be new everstept Battery Near Sercont. No more 2/12 and 12/23 of Engineers became	
	18		Front normal. Enemy artillery my quiet. Signallers report Germans seen entering SLAG ALLEY. We did not fire all day. Instructions for move out to Battern. Received instructions that 1 officer and 2 signallers per battery will attend on the 19th from the relieving Battern.	
	19.		The front was normal. The enemy shelled our support trench at intervals. He attacked on behind our lines. The enemy brought down one of our aeroplanes at 11 a.m. St. Alexandre for morning Battery. 1/10 Put gun in new billing below in Vermelles and reported 9 people Retaliated with 56 rounds. Retaliated with 45 rds on French trench.
1/11th Shook morning Battery Open target in lane with 21 rds. Sg Craig gassed on trench with 10 rounds	

WAR DIARY or INTELLIGENCE SUMMARY

Army Form C. 2118

1/4th LONDON HOWITZER BRIGADE

(Erase heading not required.)

Instructions regarding War Diaries and Intelligence Summaries are contained in F.S. Regs., Part II. and the Staff Manual respectively. Title Pages will be prepared in manuscript.

Place	Date	Hour	Summary of Events and Information	Remarks and references to Appendices
VERMELLES	FEB 20		Front Quiet. Six Enemy Balloons observed. Hostile Aeroplanes observed 8.30 am, 9.30 am, 10.15 am, and 10.55 am and 11.40 am. Aeroplane was heard on Battery (H/q) at about midnight — some slight- Zeppelin. In the morning reported that Aeroplane dropped lights on Bethune. Announcement made to move on 22nd to Esquerdiegnes near LILLERS. Inversion of 1st Corps observed on ANNEQUIN Rd. 1/4th Report all quiet. 9.0 pm.	
		1.40 pm	1/4th Battery given order "Action"- impossible to trace author of the order. Parties sent down were to see if anyone had tapped on report anything unusual.	
			1/4th fired 8 rounds on M.Gemplacements in Trench 59¢ Sip. also 8 Rnd same target.	
		1/10.15	15 " Potsdam Trench and trench near Guarrin.	
	21.		In the morning front Normal. At 1 pm onwards shot out heavier, 1/10, 96 rounds ant 59½ Sup 80 Rounds. All fired on trenches. At 1.35 Enemy kept us down on 8 of our Aeroplanes. At 3 pm very heavy bombardment burst in direction of Loos. This continued until about 5 pm when it slackened down and finally ceased about 7 pm in sight of intermittent burst of fire. At 4 pm a section of the new R.A.C. arrived at FOUQUIERES. New Battery Officer arrive at Battery Positions. On most Afrn. left at 9 pm for new Battery area. 8 Enemy Division Balloons observed. About 3 pm a very heavy bombardment was commenced evidently near Loos (south) and continued till about 8 am. This Offen closes at 12 noon on the 22nd.	

WAR DIARY
or
INTELLIGENCE SUMMARY
(Erase heading not required.)

Army Form C. 2118

Instructions regarding War Diaries and Intelligence Summaries are contained in F.S. Regs, Part II. and the Staff Manual respectively. Title Pages will be prepared in manuscript.

Place	Date	Hour	Summary of Events and Information	Remarks and references to Appendices
VERMELLES	22	10am	Left position and marched to ~~Esquerdeques~~ ECQUEDECQUES. BEF Batteries arrived same day.	
ECQUEDECQUES	23		Picked up gun near Battery B/67 RFA and put on our strength from that date.	
		10am	A.D.V.S. inspected all horses of the Brigade. All horses were mal-put same day. Junior at RELY	
	24		Telegram received from his Reg saying all leave stopped. Junior Lopt Aldridge W. Roo 1/1 Bty recommended of 2.0 p.m. Trial of Court martial - (Break in line of March).	
	25		Exterin for Pont Remy. Sunning and fueging.	
	26		Brigade Billeted as follows. Bde Hqs, Ammn Col, and B/67 Batteries 1/4 Belfontaine, and 1/10 GRANSART Orders to move on 27th received late on night of 26th.	
	27	7.30 am	Start	
		10 m	from through BELLE FONTAINE	
		12 noon	LONGPRE	
		2.30pm	DOMART	
		3.45	Airries BERNEUIL. Billet had been arranged with ASC and RAMC 46 Division. ML THIBAULT (interpret) attached 7Ab Hqs. 2 Mon left Blank in BAILLEUL with MO made arrangement with 1/4 ambulance to collect them.	
	28		Court martial of Junior Sgt Aldridge ~~continued~~ at 2.30pm - Sentence about Three late. opened on 29th	
	29		Court martial of Junior Sgt Aldridge took place. 46th Division Exam here. Weather Milder - Whole front.	

A. Shannaungh
LIEUT.-COL. R.F.A.
COMMANDING 1/4th LONDON HOWITZER BRIGADE

C.R.H.A.,
Cavalry Corps.

Having been informed by Cavalry Corps that your War Diary for the Dismounted Division will be rendered by you direct to G.S. Cavalry Corps, I enclose herewith all the War Diaries of Artillery which were in my file. Please acknowledge receipt hereon.

R M Osborne.

Captain.
General Staff.
1st Cavalry Division.

GENERAL STAFF
G.S.38/2
1 9 FEB. 1916
1ST CAVALRY DIVISION

General Staff,
Cavalry Corps.

Herewith War Diary for
H.Q. Dismounted Divisional Artillery.
1/4th London R.F.A. (Howitzers).
from January 1st to February 21st 1916.

H.Q. Artillery,
Dismounted Division.
22/2/16.

Bde. Major,
Dismounted Division Artillery.

CONFIDENTIAL.

WAR DIARY

1/4 LONDON HOWITZER BRIGADE R.F.A.

1st MARCH 1916 - 31st MARCH 1916.

Vol VI

Army Form C. 2118

WAR DIARY or INTELLIGENCE SUMMARY

(Erase heading not required.)

1/4" London Howitzer Bde R.F.A.

Instructions regarding War Diaries and Intelligence Summaries are contained in F.S. Regs., Part II. and the Staff Manual respectively. Title Pages will be prepared in manuscript.

Place	Date	Hour	Summary of Events and Information	Remarks and references to Appendices
BERNEUIL	1.3.1916	10 a.m	Major Brownrigg Shute and C.R.A. 56" Divn visited 1/5 Brigade. Bathing & running. 3 J.C.O's and 16 men arrived from the Base.	
	2.3.1916	—	On Parley to Lullaine. 5th Brigade left & transferred from London for Boulogne. Brigade signalling class ran. 2nd & 3rd supervision visited. Personnel drawn from 5/E.C.M. for Lipt Eldridge 1/5 Bdy. Baggage begins returned to A.S.C. Bathing & running.	
	3.3.1916		Fine day. Nothing to report. Bathing & running. Brigade signalling class.	
	4.3.1916		Snowed heavily. Bathing & running. Brigade signalling class.	
	5.3.1916	11 a.m 12.30 p.m	Church Parade. Burial - A.D.M.S. visited Brigade.	
	6.3.1916		Cold day. Nothing to report. Brigade signalling class.	
	7.3.1916	10 a.m 10.30 a.m	C.R.A. 56" Divn visited 1/5 Brigade. Bathing Hot bath. Brigade of Inspired 1/11 Battery Hot bath. Brigade signalling class.	
	8.3.1916	10.30 a.m	A.D.M.S. called to inspect Men for fumigated Bath week. Bathing & running. Brigade signalling class.	
	9.3.1916	2 p.m	S.A.A. Section from 56" Div Ammunition Column joined 1/5 Brigade. Strength arrived - 9 drivers, 18 L.D. horses, 3 G.S. wagons. 64 trays of S.A.A. and 64 trays of grenades. Bathing & running. Brigade signalling class.	
	10.3.1916		Fine day. Nothing to report. Bathing & running. Brigade signalling class. Examined nine J 2nd & 3rd class supervision.	
	11.3.1916		Duties noticed for Church service.	
	12.3.1916	8.30 a.m	Brigade left BERNEUIL for new billeting area "OCCOCHES". Advance party from "OCCOCHES" already transferred by Troops. Via to Division Billeting in relation to OUTREBOIS and ammunition column at "OCCOCHES". Area south of line 2" AUTHIE.	
		11 a.m	Brigade arrived in new area. Billets sufficient pony lines and wagon park.	
OUTREBOIS	13.3.1916	10.30 a.m	C.R.A. 56" Divn visited Brigade. Early modern Orderly Officers sent to BERNEUIL to investigate Claims. Major Birchell left for Orderly Officers sent to hop skimmed bars.	
	14.3.1916	10.30 a.m 2.30 p.m	C.R.A. 56" Divn visited Brigade. Major Birchell left for England to take command of a unit in England. Party left for new billeting area. French interpreter for Command received.	

W: W593/826 1,000,000 4/15 J.B.C. & A. A.D.S.S./Forms/C. 2118.

WAR DIARY
or
INTELLIGENCE SUMMARY
(Erase heading not required.)

Army Form C. 2118

1/4 London Howitzer Brigade R.F.A.

Place	Date	Hour	Summary of Events and Information	Remarks and references to Appendices
OUTREBOIS WAMIN – ROZIERE	15.3.16	9 a.m. 1 p.m.	Brigade left OUTREBOIS for new billeting area WAMIN – ROZIERE. Weather wet, roads good. New billets in very bad condition.	
	16.3.16		Orders received for Brigade Badges to report in writing to the Brown Officer. Cleaning up billets. Building loaned as an armoury.	
	17.3.16	10.30 a.m.	C.R.A. 56th Div visits Brigade. 6 men from Ammn Col on temporary posted to 1/11 Battery. Clearing up billets.	
	18.3.16	9 a.m. 11 a.m. 11 a.m. 12 noon	C.O. Brigade, Captain Bankwell sent to see Gnl Sanders. C.R.A. 14th Brun. 5 Officers and 30 men sent Bonpareli attn 56th Divn at RESERVE. End of Gunnery in his house and from R.A.C. 2nd Paget C.R.A. II Corps visits Brigade Office. Cleaning up billets.	
	19.3.16	7 a.m. 10.30 a.m. 11 a.m.	Church Service from WAMIN, Church by British our friends. Parade Service at ROZIERE. C.R.A. 56th Divn visits Brigade. Cleaning up billets.	
	20.3.16	10.30 a.m. 11 a.m.	Presentation by C.O. Brigade of Hyp Staff 1/10 Battery in F.S.M.O. C.R.A. 56th Divn called, and left kit of material at R.E. dumps.	
	21.3.16	3 p.m.	Taught by H.C.M.C. to Brigade Smith Hyp Staff to Supersaw alarm Hyp Staff. Battery Gunnery. Supervision Alarm. Hyp Staff ammunition.	
	22.3.16	11.30 a.m.	2.21 F.A.C. Inspection required to Brigade from Depo 56 Div Artly. Adjt left on 7 days leave to England. Battery training. Signs Alarm Class Hyp Staff.	
	23.3.16	9.30 a.m. 10.30 a.m. 11 a.m.	Brown d Sgln & F.C.M.O. 2nd Smith Inspection by C.O. Brigade of 1/11 Bhy in F.S.M.O. Capt Scotland and 2.N. Braw for trenching. Crew of Gunnery in Court of horse teaming to B.A.C. Signalling Class Hyp Staff.	
	24.3.16		Gale of wind in early morning. Battery. Brigade Signalling Classes.	
	25.3.16	9.30 a.m.	1/11 Battery send 1. A.S. Hamilton, 1 woaken and 1 gunner to Artillery School, HAUTECLOQUE. Capt Dunsmith returned from leave from Hyp VI Corps R.A. Battery training. B du Hyp Signalling Polner.	
	26.3.16	9.30 a.m. 10 a.m.	Capt Gray, 2nd Lieutn. 26 Inspection and Behn Ops Stevens. Opl Gragg left to join Artillery School HAUTECLOQUE. C.R.A. 56th Div. called.	

1875 Wt W593/826 1,000,000 4/15 J.B.C. & A. A.D.S.S./Forms/C. 2118.

Army Form C. 2118

WAR DIARY
or
INTELLIGENCE SUMMARY
(Erase heading not required.)

1/1L London Howitzer Brigade. R.F.A.

Place	Date	Hour	Summary of Events and Information	Remarks and references to Appendices
WAMIN - ROZIERE	27.3.16		Bde. ord. Brigade staff superintending showers. Battery training.	
	28.3.16	10.30am 11.30am	C.O. inspected Brigade ammunition column in F.S.M.O. C.R.A. called. Brigade staff superintending showers. Battery training.	
	29.3.16	9.15am	C.O. up the line with C.R.A. Battery training. Brig. de Off. superintending showers.	
	30.3.16	10.30am	Lt. Bulloch 1/11 Battery went on leave. ditto Commander in Chief accompanied by Lt. Matthews passed through front of 1/11 Battery area. Battery training. Brig. de staff superintending showers.	
	31.3.16		A rainy day. Nothing to report.	

[signature] Lt. Col. R.F.A.
Commanding 1/4th London Howitzer Brigade

WAR DIARY
or
INTELLIGENCE SUMMARY

1/4TH LONDON HOWITZER BRIGADE.

Place	Date	Hour	Summary of Events and Information	Remarks and references to Appendices
WAMIN.	April 1		R.S.M. WILEY, left for home establishment. – Struck off strength. B.S.M. Robinson appointed A/R.S.M vice Wiley	
	2		Nothing to report.	
	3		C.O. appointed Town Commandant for ROZIERE and BROUILLY. O.C. Apprentice Procured to Court Martial at PREVENT. TELEGRAM received "All leave stopped"	
	4		Nothing to report	
	5		Nothing to report	
	6		Adv. recent Ret R Battery to go up into the line. Court Martial held sitting on 82 and forward. Captain Deane A.V.C. went on leave.	
	7		R Battery went into action, left billet here at 9.15am. the section of Ammo Col. accompanied them. The Payn and CRA received notice of Bmjate at 10.40 am. Capt Gray 2i/c batten and fignmen returned from Artillery School. (R Battery attached to 47th Bmj/de R.F.A. – 14 division	
	8		16 Remounts received and taken on strength of Brigade	
	9		Officer and men (return) attended Artillery School. Officers attended exhibition of Flammenwerfer. 18 NCOs and men reported for duty and were taken on the strength.	
	10		Officers joined and were posted as follows Lt Boruth 11/10 RFA, 2/Lt Darlington, Amm Col, and 2/Lt Lutnidge to 1/11L. Also 10 men for duty and taken on Stgth	
	11		2/Lt H Kennington reported for duty	
	12		C.O. (Lt Hannington R.H.A) went on leave	
	13		Nothing to report	
	14		Recd adv all leave stopped by 18/5. Wird to Lt Hannington to return, all OC's warned. 2/Lt Kennington attached to R Battery.	
	15		Nothing to report	

WAR DIARY
or
INTELLIGENCE SUMMARY

(Erase heading not required.)

Instructions regarding War Diaries and Intelligence Summaries are contained in F.S. Regs., Part II. and the Staff Manual respectively. Title Pages will be prepared in manuscript.

Place	Date	Hour	Summary of Events and Information	Remarks and references to Appendices
WAMIN	16		Church Parade 9.30 am	
			Maur C.R.A. and Brigade Major and Signalling Officer called	
	17		C.R.A. called. 12 Signallers went to Div Signalling School. Captain Adams MC returned from leave. Received cheque from Messrs Potter for francs 1439.70 – sent on to O.C. 1/10 Batt.	
	18		Lt Wainwright returned from leave 7 pm	
	19		Officers went up the line to inspect gun position	
	20		Lt Wainwright went to St Pol to take command of "Senior Officers Course", Acting Officer accompanied him	
	21		Maur returned from Artillery School	
	22		Col Wainwright (C.O) called	
	23		Maunt Birch to make reconnaissance (200?) Course front at Hinchlynes Arty School – 10 Officers and 1 NCO	
	24		Nothing to report	
	25		Gun truck started (200?) Brigade signalling class restarted	
	26		4 Officers went to Line to inspect gun position	
	27		Nothing to report	
	28		Major W Ridge returned from England and reported for duty. C.O Returned from St Pol	
	29		Officers attended reconnaissance at Div School Lionecky. C.O returned to St Pol	
	30		Nothing to report	
			During the month Chalk was drawn and foundations to truck standings laid down if every unit. Each unit also built truck recesses.	

Morris Major FOR LIEUT.-COL.
COMMANDING 4th LONDON (HOWITZER) BRIGADE, R.F.A.

56/~~40~~ ~~Offensive R.A. Section~~
           ~~3rd Echelon~~

283RD BRIGADE R.F.A.
late 1/4 London Bde

WAR DIARY

For MAY, 1916

CONFIDENTIAL

283rd BRIGADE R.F.A.

WAR DIARY or INTELLIGENCE SUMMARY

Army Form C. 2118

Place	Date	Hour	Summary of Events and Information	Remarks and references to Appendices
WAMIN	MAY 1	—	Fire broke out in 1/2nd London Bde Area. Alarm given at 9.30 am. All in diamond 9.45 am. No importance. Nothing further to report.	
"	2	—	100 blankets sent to be fumigated. Buy Mare. No.19, H.Q. Staff, died of Ruptured Stomach — V.O. in attendance.	
"	3	—	Chestnut Mare No.14, H.Q. Staff, died of Ruptured Stomach — V.O. in attendance. Nothing further to report.	
"	4	—	Details recd. for March to PAS on 8th, from Divnl. H.Q. A.D.M.S. called.	
"	5	—	March orders recd from 56th Divn. Arty, also details of Billeting Areas. Divn. Arty H.Q. moves to HENU. C.O. & Orderly Officer returned from Senior Officers' School at ST. POL, where C.O. 1/14th Ldn. How. Bde was in charge.	
"	6	—	Conference at Bde H.Q. of Battery Commdrs. Received Route March Orders from O.C. 1/14th Ldn. Bde. R.F.A.	
"	7	—	Further Orders received. Notified we are to relieve 48th Division. 1/111th Battery receive gun back from Artillery School.	
PAS	8	—	Arrive at PAS. Go into tents.	
"	9	—	Nothing to report.	
"	10	—	Lt. Col. Wainwright appointed Area Commandant, PAS HUTS. M.O. went on leave.	
"	11	—	1/10th Battery went into line. Grouped under Col. McDowell, commanding London Group Artillery. A/R.S.M. E.G Robinson returned from months leave.	

Army Form C. 2118

WAR DIARY
or
INTELLIGENCE SUMMARY
(Erase heading not required.)

Instructions regarding War Diaries and Intelligence Summaries are contained in F.S. Regs., Part II. and the Staff Manual respectively. Title Pages will be prepared in manuscript.

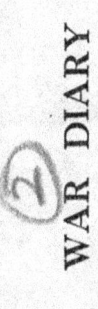

Place	Date	Hour	Summary of Events and Information	Remarks and references to Appendices
PAS	MAY 12	-	Commenced drawing material from R.E. for completing gun emplacements & dug-outs at HÉBUTERNE. Name of Brigade changed to 283rd BRIGADE, R.F.A. from 1/4th LONDON HOW. BDE R.F.A. Designation of Batteries changed from 1/10th, 1/11th, and "R", to "A", "B", "C", respectively. Major W. Bridges returns to England under War Office Orders to command a Brigade R.F.A.	
"	13	-	Drew material from R.E. 1/R.S.M. Robinson went up to line to commence work on dug-outs for H.Q. Staff, with 6 H.Q. Staff men and 15 men from 56th D.A.C.	
"	14	-	Nothing to report.	
"	15	-	Drew material from R.E. 2/Lt. Remington to report to Trench Mortar School. 2/Lt. Edgson went up to line to commence work on gun-pits for C/283rd Battery.	
"	16	-	Drew further material from R.E. Heavy bombardment of HÉBUTERNE at about 3 a.m. Received urgent call from A/283rd Battery for 4 wagons of ammunition at 3.15 a.m. These left at once.	
"	17	-	B.A.C. taken over by D.A.C. Adjt. interviewed Major Parker, R.E., & also Lt. Williamson, R.E. (1/1st Edinboro') with reference to material for gun-pits. Also called at Div. Arty. H.Q. to see Brig-Gen. Elkington.	
"	18	-	Orders received for Capt. Adjt. Adams, A.V.C. to join D.A.C. Nothing further to report.	
"	19	-	C.R.A. called at PAS. Nothing further to report.	
"	20	-	Court-Martial held at Bde. H.Q. at 11 a.m. President - O.C. 283rd Bde. R.F.A.	
"	21	-	C.O. & Adjt. went up line. Called on O.C. LONDON GROUP ARTILLERY. Met C.R.A. Also saw Genl. Allenby in HÉBUTERNE	

APPENDIX "A"

C O P Y.

Officer Commanding,
    283rd Brigade, R.F.A.

S/CRA/179.
26/5/16.

    In continuation of this Office No.S/CRA/179, dated 16/5/16, the re-organization of the 56th Divisional Artillery will be carried out forthwith.

    The following will be the necessary transfers :-

A/283 Bty. will become D/281 on transfer to 281 Bde.

B/283 Bty.   "   "   D/280 on   "   " 280 "

C/283 Bty.   "   "   D/282 on   "   " 282 "

D/280 Bty.   "   "   A/283 on   "   " 283 "

D/281 Bty.   "   "   B/283 on   "   " 283 "

D/282 Bty.   "   "   C/283 on   "   " 283 "

    The three "D" Batteries of the 18 Pdr. Brigades coming under the Headquarters of the 283rd Brigade and the three Howitzer Batteries being transferred as shewn above.

                          sd/ BRUCE MACMIN, Captain,
                          Staff Captain, R.A.
26/5/16.   56th Division.

WAR DIARY or INTELLIGENCE SUMMARY

Army Form C. 2118

(Erase heading not required.)

Instructions regarding War Diaries and Intelligence Summaries are contained in F.S. Regs., Part II. and the Staff Manual respectively. Title Pages will be prepared in manuscript.

Place	Date	Hour	Summary of Events and Information	Remarks and references to Appendices
PAS.	MAY 22	—	Nothing to report.	
"	23	—	A.D.C. 56th Division, & C.R.A. inspected camp. Nothing further to report.	
"	24	—	Nothing to report	
"	25	—	Nothing to report.	
"	26	—	Ordered to split up Brigade forthwith, as per G.H.Q letter No O.B.818. (Vide Appendix A.) O.C. 283rd Bde. R.F.A. takes over command of LONDON GROUP from O.C. 281st Bde.	
"	27	—	Nothing to report.	
SAILLY-AU-BOIS	28	1 pm	Adjt and Staff go up to line to take over Office of LONDON GROUP ARTILLERY. Enemy = D/280, D/281, J/P/282 Batteries taken over. A/283, B/283, C/283 posted to 281 & 282 Bdes respectively. All rounds 75 & 18lb. 283 Battery at intervals with 77 mm. Still.	
"	29	11 am	An organised shoot was carried out at 11am on enemy "STRONG POINT". Heavies co-operated. We fired 219 rds. altogether. F.O.O.s report good effect. We retaliated several times during the day for hostile fire on our trenches near HÉBUTERNE	
"	30	12.12am	Retaliation called for by Infantry. We immediately barraged the front line trenches, & fired off altogether 164 rds. "Cease fire" was given at 12.45am.	
		2.34am	"S.O.S." call was received. All Batteries opened fire at once. After several rapid bursts the interval was increased, and a steady rate of fire was maintained on night lines until 3 am, when an order from 169th Inf. Bde. came through to "stop firing". We fired approximately 276 rds.	

Army Form C. 2118

WAR DIARY
or
INTELLIGENCE SUMMARY
(Erase heading not required.)

Instructions regarding War Diaries and Intelligence Summaries are contained in F. S. Regs., Part II. and the Staff Manual respectively. Title Pages will be prepared in manuscript.

Place	Date	Hour	Summary of Events and Information	Remarks and references to Appendices
SAILLY au-BOIS (contd).	MAY 30	11.40pm	"S.O.S" received through 169th Inf. Bde. All guns opened fire instantly, and ceased firing at 11.55pm. 108 rds were fired altogether. This "S.O.S" recd came from advanced posts in new trenches.	
"	31.	11.15am	Two suspected Trench Mortars were engaged by order of G.O.C. 169th Inf. Bde. 8 rounds were fired. Desultory hostile shelling & trench mortaring during the day, but nothing of importance occurred.	

A.H.Barrewright
Lt. Col. R.F.A.
Commanding 283rd Brigade R.F.A.

L 283 BRIGADE R.F.A.

CONFIDENTIAL
Army Form C. 2118

283 (I)
2½ Bde R.F.A.

56

WAR DIARY
or
INTELLIGENCE SUMMARY
(Erase heading not required.)

Instructions regarding War Diaries and Intelligence Summaries are contained in F.S. Regs., Part II. and the Staff Manual respectively. Title Pages will be prepared in manuscript.

Place	Date	Hour	Summary of Events and Information	Remarks and references to Appendices
SAILLY	June 1		Some shelling during the early morning. Weather on the front quieter.	
			About 60 sight shells sent over a battery position (about 5 pdrs?) in Bn Sinister Battery fired at about	
			3 p.m. Ply sec.	
		10.30 pm	Mortar Code received from Bde O.P.	
		10.?	Bethne entered + fired at O.P.	
			S.O.S. from Infantry. At 10.15 were alarmed carrying Infantry Patrol were out.	
		10.35	Mortar Code received again from Bde part down. Batteries ordered to fire by F.O.O.	
		10.??	Battle fire.	
		10.41	S.O.S. received from 0.3 D/283. 266 Batteries fired at once. Fire of twos to have seen a flare alarm	
			after the S.O.S. Rocket signal was seen.	
		10.50	Infantry raised report all quiet.	
	June 2	about 3 am	About 150 rounds shown on our front line trenches to retaliation enemy trench mortars. Enemy fired 15 sighters in our trench tampering huns quiet. C.R.A. arrived at 10 am	
		10.30 am	To check on Battery position at D/283. Ro comm? ? ? communication to a track RLI ?	
		? am	Any agree of Infantry A/281 ?? fired a few rounds H.E. on an Ordnance Sup dump mere interesting	
		? pm	team trenches. Evening much quiet.	
	June 3	1.30 am	Infantry patrol sent to establish to French trench. 1.30 fired 12 rounds on sentry post.	
		1.55 am	A/281 - 6 rounds on trench june line at K.M.E.9.?	
		2.0 am	Heavy trench mortaring in progress. Infantry assault from Lozago 9/21.	
		3.20 am	on ? A/281 battalion well ? fire on trench ??	
		2.30 pm	C.R.A. over.	
		10 pm onwards	H/2 Bbt here opened about 12 guns intermittent ? on one ?	
			I.O withheld during the night as intended on French trench.	

1875 Wt. W593/826 1,000,000 4/15 J.B.C. & A. A.D.S.S./Forms/C. 2118.

Army Form C. 2118

WAR DIARY
or
INTELLIGENCE SUMMARY
(Erase heading not required.)

Instructions regarding War Diaries and Intelligence Summaries are contained in F.S. Regs., Part II. and the Staff Manual respectively. Title Pages will be prepared in manuscript.

Place	Date	Hour	Summary of Events and Information	Remarks and references to Appendices
CHLY	June 4	10 p. 12 noon	Aeroplane shot down at 10 a.m. B/153 had shots at 150 H.E. at 12 & 2.2 due practice. Not shots fired at several on various Ronnie mortars	
		11.35 p.m.	Enemy D/17 was sufficient to answer. Reg Hgrs. 1/157.A & 12-guns H.E. on B/223, Y/17 + regist + R.V.C. infantry.	
	5	12.30 a.m.	A.S.R. Enemy Division to Bns y 4 mins offering on North North Night shells. 'tic' [?] shelling, shrapnel & H.E. at [?] on way to Bn Hq. B/153 fits. No hands fired. 3/127 1/7 Bde.	
		9 p.m.-2 p.m.	Ravine shrapnel	
		7.5 pm	13 rounds on Ronnie Juncture. 6.2 5 m	
	6		Not rounds fired [?] not 7 [?] rear trench. 5.0.5 Barrage started at 10.20 pm. Enemy very [?] shelling, [?] intervals at 8 pm and 3/4 sent in casualties.	
	7	10.30 C.E.	4 o'clock. Intervention of Chq [?] that 20 Turk were seen & attempt running from Baalbeck trench to Bughaman. Nos known.	
	8		Patrol at 10 am and at 12 m.	
	9	8.30 3 pm	Lint 2 mortar fire to the open. Prepared Draper Poisinties. Dismount of relention shells. Ryll trent. Vl. Col. called at 4 pm.	
	10	1am 11.35 12 c	Enemy Aeroplanes flew South. R.V.C. infantry Grenade attack prepared on Y.So. After D/2er 85 rpnds 2 und. a colt. Munim fad our shot and rocket.	

1875. Wt. W.593/826 1,000,000 4/15 I.B.C. & A. A.D.S.S./Forms/C. 2118.

Army Form C. 2118

Instructions regarding War Diaries and Intelligence Summaries are contained in F.S. Regs., Part II. and the Staff Manual respectively. Title Pages will be prepared in manuscript.

WAR DIARY
or
INTELLIGENCE SUMMARY
(Erase heading not required.)

Place	Date June	Hour	Summary of Events and Information	Remarks and references to Appendices
SAILLY	11	7.55 a.m.	Infantry ordered to retaliation at V.S.S area. Enemy at Bethune. C.T.E. to relieve. Patrol of men reported near PETTENCY FARM.	
PAS	12		Col. Bastinell arrived at 11 am. he returned to PAS at 4 pm. Adv party Officers and 7 rising other ranks taken to billets.	
	13		Col. Wainwright went to live at Bn HQ at Henu.	
	14		Nothing to report.	
	15		Bn moved to HENU & 12 noon (in 2&3 Bde)	
HENU	16		Nothing to report.	
	17		Advs Officers returned from Sailly. Signallers [crossed out] remain to the front.	
	18		Nothing to report	
	19		Nothing to report.	
	20		Suz watcher returns. Enemy shelled on the Battn unsuccessfuly.	
	21		Nothing to report	
	22		Nothing to report	
	23		Nothing to report.	
	24		V.Amy. Bombardment Starts. B.H. HQts moves in subways as Battnson etc proposed.	

1875 Wt. W593/826 1,000,000 4/15 J.B.C. & A. A.D.S.S./Forms/C. 2118.

Army Form C. 2118

WAR DIARY
or
INTELLIGENCE SUMMARY
(Erase heading not required.)

Instructions regarding War Diaries and Intelligence Summaries are contained in F. S. Regs., Part II. and the Staff Manual respectively. Title Pages will be prepared in manuscript.

Place	Date	Hour	Summary of Events and Information	Remarks and references to Appendices
HENU.	June 25		Nothing to report	
	26		" " "	
	27		" " "	
	28		" " "	
	29		" " "	
	30			

(ORIGINAL)

To 56th Divisional Artillery.

WAR DIARY OF

283rd BRIGADE R.F.A
(& CENTRE GROUP)
FOR

JULY, 1916.

CONFIDENTIAL

ORIGINAL

283rd BRIGADE R.F.A.

CENTRE GROUP

WAR DIARY
or
INTELLIGENCE SUMMARY
(Erase heading not required.)

Army Form C. 2118.

283rd BRIGADE, R.F.A.

No. AF.49
to Appendices
Date 3/1/16

Instructions regarding War Diaries and Intelligence Summaries are contained in F.S. Regs., Part II. and the Staff Manual respectively. Title pages will be prepared in manuscript.

ALL MAP REFERENCES ON MAP 1:10,000 57D NE. SHEETS {1 and 2, 3 and 4} PARTS

Hour, Date, Place	Summary of Events and Information	Remarks and references
July 1,2,3,4,5,6,7 HENU	Nothing to Report.	
8,9,10	Laying wire to connect Bty to near Central Group Hqs at Chateau la Haie.	
11 Chateau de la HAIE	Moved to Chateau de la HAIE	
12/13	Took over Front at 6 p.m. Relieved 2 Div Ark and also Infty Bde Hqs. Communication to all Btys, Battalion Hqs and Coy Commandant complete. The front party guns. Some activity on part of T.M's. 10g². 5F attached in request of infantry. (E.27.C.) Rt. Bty of new Sandbag guns at K.4.D.25.80. Btt. of Lts.F wire at (K.4.D.3.4) reenforced X.A.47.3.	
10.15 p.m.	3 Blue rockets east of FONQUEVILLERS. Enemy hostile along parapet at E.30.A.4.4.	
	3 German Balloons up. No Aeroplanes.	
13/14 10 pm to 8 am.	Organized Bombardment carried out by Div Bty. Very little retaliation from 12.25–12.45. Enemy repeat M.G sent up red rocket. Some tear shells fell at 1.35 a.m. at R.F.A.	
	Shining day. 93rd and 109² Cut wires. No Balloons. Aircraft active.	
	No find about 4000 rounds in Bombardment.	
14/15 do	Very very quiet. Light tod. Aircraft retali. nil. It near connecte work repaired	
(14) 6.45 p.m.	at K.3.d.F½.9½. + German seen working at Horse E.27.C.7. OT.	
	109¹ and 93 85. Cutting wire.	

WAR DIARY or INTELLIGENCE SUMMARY

Army Form C. 2118.

Hour, Date, Place	Summary of Events and Information	Remarks and references to Appendices
July		
15/16. Chateau la Haie	C.R.A. Called. 2/Lt Carr from 109th to R.A.C. Lt Blunn from R.A.C. to 109th Bty. Day very quiet. Hversation Baz. Weather misty. 20. 5.9 shells our strong point P in K.3.A. 93rd, 109th and C/253 Btys cut wire. Red rockets shown in direction of SERRE during night.	
16/17. "	C.R.A called. Enemy fairly quiet. Shelled our lines SAILLY in afternoon. Enemy Infantry Brigade extended their front to the North. C/252 Carrs reversed their Group on the 17th inst.. We carried out a bombardment (1000 rounds per Group) in conjunction with infantry raids. Enemy retaliated on our trenches. Raids given enemy very good. 93, 109th + C/253 cut wire.	
17/18. "	C.R.A. Called. We carried out special bombardment during night. (Group Per Bn) (3 rounds) Hor Bty D/252. Practically no retaliation. 2. 77mm Shells on Chateau La Haie – D/250 attached to us instead.	
18/19. "	Hostile artillery generally more active. A certain amount of T.M. activity reported. 5. 9 (about 50) scattered over the front front also about 150 77mm and 4.2.s. shrunken fairly quiet. 3 Hostile Balloons up.	
19/20. "	C.R.A. Called. Enemy trench mining at E.28.d.2.7 appears to have been extended to E.28.D.05.75. Also new trench dug from E.28.B.07.05 to E.28.D.3.80. 109th + 93rd Btys. cut wire. Hostile artillery fairly quiet. No believed no hostile attempt shown.	

WAR DIARY or INTELLIGENCE SUMMARY.

Army Form C. 2118.

(3)

Hour, Date, Place	Summary of Events and Information	Remarks and references to Appendices
JULY		
20/21. Château la Haie	Enemy artillery generally more active. Our trench were shelled during the day with 4.2 and 5.9 shells. Aeroplane arrived at 11 a.m. to register targets. Too misty, aeroplane returned.	
6.0 pm	Aeroplane returned, registered target for 93 Bty. M.6.45.77 (Fair) message was received and all batteries who could reach target engaged it.	
7.45 to 12 n.n	Enemy shelling Nothing Copy Ballery in E.26.A. with 5.9's. About 200.	
9.15 to 10 a.m	Jo aeroplane - reformalf null 200 fired a number of rounds on German line. North Aeroplane over FONQUEVILLERS at about 11 a.m.	
	2nd Lieut Hay reported for duty from Base, posted to 109th Bty.	
	Lt Brewer from 109th to 93 Bty. Lt Pugh Hampton to C.C.S. (Neuville rue) Corps Commander called.	
	S/n Lieut Grant D/250 to fire 50 rounds with ESSARTS at 10 a.m.	
21/22	North artillery fairly active. E21, E26, E27 shelled by 5.9's at 11 a.m. (11) FONQUEVILLERS shelled by 5.9's. Barrway demolished. T.M.'s also fairly active. 9.3's and 10.9's cut wire	
10 a.m	F.R artillerie 109's and C/223 Brigade Royal wire. Aeroplane	

Army Form C. 2118.

WAR DIARY
or
INTELLIGENCE SUMMARY.
(Erase heading not required.)

Instructions regarding War Diaries and Intelligence Summaries are contained in F.S. Regs., Part II. and the Staff Manual respectively. Title pages will be prepared in manuscript.

Hour, Date, Place	Summary of Events and Information	Remarks and references to Appendices
JULY		
22/23 12.30	Giant pineapple arr at K.3.d.9½.9½. This target was engaged by one of our 18 pdr batt[erie]s	
2 pm	Hostile T.M. very active. Position of T.M. K.5.C.05.20.	
3 pm	FONQUEVILLERS was again shelled by 4.2 and 5.9s	
1 am	Heavy machine gun fire from opposite FONQUEVILLERS during the night. Heavy bombardment activity on the South. It was considered very noticeable during the night	
8 am	T.M. active. Emmenwerfer fired on Y56. We retaliated on N.H. & 9½. Emmenwerfer	
10.30 am	No activ[it]y at the present. Persicope observed at K.3.a.9½.9½. Trench mortar seen at K.3.d.9.7.	
	Hostile aircraft Nil. Light Nil. Suspected M.G. emplacement at ɛ.28.d.05.90.	
23/24 7.15 pm	Hostile trenchmortar active from K.5.c.7.3 – Smoke shown at x.4.a.6.3. K.4.c.9.4. K.4.d.2.5.	
	Lights were observed from K.4.d.16. to X.4.d.9.5. The front was not normal	
	Some aircraft activity, 3 machine flew over our front. One machine dropped	
	a white light. A nest emplacement observed at ɛ.28.D.05.90. Trench just into it	
	Great quiet. Hostile trench mortar at FOE trench nose farm. A new trench appears	
24/V	to have run from K.11.a.4.9 to K.5.c.2.1.	
	Work appeared to be going on in GOMMECOURT Church	

WAR DIARY or INTELLIGENCE SUMMARY

Army Form C. 2118.

Hour, Date, Place	Summary of Events and Information	Remarks and references to Appendices
25/26. 1.30 p.m.	Percuta Fleurea at K.4.K.35.85. C.R.A. called.	
2.10 p.m.	Working Party shewed E.2.E.D.2.C. They were fired on by Sniper Rifle.	
2.58 p.m.	German Officer shewed enemy at E.2.F.B.15.10. — Enemy fired Rifle Grenade from 6 p.m. Government Park. — Machine gun active during night junction F.7 and F.N.D.	
	One German firer from K.5.C.70.30. F. K.5.C.50.35.	
26/27.	C.R.A. Called. Dark quiet. Look going on in ration parties of Essex Brigade. Three FOKKER aeroplanes flew at great height over TORQUENTOTERS. One machine	
	unchanged several rockets. One of our aeroplanes dropped a white rocket on K.1.Sub.5.	
	Night quiet. Thick mist.	
27/28.	Stay arrived. Sixth aeroplane patrolled very high. Thick mist every morning and	
	early morning. C.R.A. Called.	
28/29.	Considerably more activity in the air than usual. Enemy aeroplanes patrolled the line mostly flying low behind their own line. S.S. from North	
	aeroplanes flying on Helston. One new burst appears to have been very	
	between EPTE at K.5.C.9.5. and FELL at K.5.C.43.	

WAR DIARY
or
INTELLIGENCE SUMMARY.

(Erase heading not required.)

Army Form C. 2118.

Hour, Date, Place	Summary of Events and Information	Remarks and references to Appendices
29/30.	A German Staff Officer spoken looking on ground X + 2 1. Enemy Aircraft fairly active during the day. British Aeroplane paid to descend in front of Sailly. Pilot wounded by machine gun bullets.	
	Our Artillery shot down well of several batteries in Gommecourt village - fells caused from the ridges. Very noisy Shenandoar far.	
30/31.	Very quiet all day on front of enemy Aeroplanes. We registered target with Aeropl Observer. C.R.A called. Enemy Snipers very active.	
	18 traces suspected of troops moved from line to Pd Public Return.	
	Relay 7 104 and c/RE3 Bg.	
	Enemy fairly active with T.M.s.	

A.M.cccccc /L.C.

LIEUT.-COL. R.F.A.
COMMANDING 173 BRIGADE

56th Divisional Artillery

283rd BRIGADE

ROYAL FIELD ARTILLERY.

AUGUST 1916

INTELLIGENCE SUMMARY

283 Bde R.F.A.

Place	Date	Hour	Summary of Events and Information	Remarks and references to Appendices
CHATEAU LA HAIE	AUGUST 1		Any quiet. Enemy's activity well N.G.'s against an aeroplane rather above normal. Ulrictown now shelled at intervals with 77's, also a few 4.2. Smoke shewed rising from portion of trench but extent of S.E. (suspected) in Government village. One attempt from concentration Tot received at 2 pm.	
	2	2 pm	Any quiet. Some activity in front of North T.M. He got a concentration Tot at noon. At about 7:30 pm an aeroplane circled the Chinese trees. Any returned within half an hour.	
	3	10 pm	He shelled enemy transport which caused a steady to nil. Presently two fires were effected in the enemy established regiment on our transport at 10:30 pm. Any quiet. Situation led C.R. L caused at Bn.Hp. At 8:45 enemy aeroplane downed	
		10:30 pm	RR cml secured from Indian trench. Any quiet. Front normal.	
	4	3:40 am	Very heavy bombardment on BIENVILLIERS. At 8:29 Arrival Bty under. 10 mins to stand by and to mor. All quiet Later Except H:30 am. Rumas reserve from hostile troops— Remarks complained of trench mortar activity, acting rally from of 5th Notts in Back anywhere very active. Autenoon and morning 93.7.85 and 98/82 shelled by C.A. 93.7 had in. One pit and put knocked out 6/82 the gun pit untouched, gun unsupport. A.W.S casualty	
	5			

2449 Wt. W14957/M90 750,000 1/16 J.B.C. & A. Forms/C.2113/12.

INTELLIGENCE SUMMARY

Instructions regarding War Diaries and Intelligence Summaries are contained in F.S. Regs., Part II and the Staff Manual respectively. Title Pages will be prepared in manuscript.

(Erase heading not required.)

Place	Date	Hour	Summary of Events and Information	Remarks and references to Appendices
CHATEAU la HAIE	AUGUST 5		Germans shelling 93? Bty appeared to be peering to be ~~around the~~ Bois Rossignol wood.	
	6	10.30 am	G.O.C. R.A. Capt. called at Group H.Q. The enemy had 3 Balloons up.	
		4 pm	During the day "Sas Ebel" was visited. Front S.G. and L.2.S. put on on trenches. The 109? registered some Target with Balloon observation. 8 notice broke was put up in the enemy lines. C. R. A. called.	
	7		We bombarded enemy trenches. French aviators cooperating. Observing runway C.R.A. called. In the afternoon Brigade trips called. Several both Balloons up. There was brisk activity at various times during the day and thus neighbourhood.	
	8		There has been a marked increase in hostile aeroplane activity. Several places were seen flying quite low in North Balloon obs. day very quiet.	
	9		C.R.A. called. He seemed to harbour misgivings from aircraft going in Target Enemy baloons 9/585 and 1098 engaged this Target. Very noisy from great. Sky camouflage as aid to support forward Advance. 937 By? received damaged from back from I.O.M. casualties except for Lieuten Aylw.	
	10		C. R. A. called. Day quiet. Nothing to report. Maybe Troops Coller.	
	11	2 am	Sudden Burst reply to F.adence T.M. that was worrying their infantry. 93? fired 3 salvoes Fired. Miss. fell ill.	

INTELLIGENCE SUMMARY

(Erase heading not required.)

Instructions regarding War Diaries and Intelligence Summaries are contained in F. S. Regs., Part II. and the Staff Manual respectively. Title Pages will be prepared in manuscript.

Place	Date	Hour	Summary of Events and Information	Remarks and references to Appendices
Chateau du ? HAIF	12		Army quiet and civil. 2'd Brind from 1045 to 11.50 over ?? front to ??????	
			2.R.B. carried from 12 to 1 1.30 pm. S.F. in sector on ?? intended to bypass close ??. Von Bryan ??? ? called. Cropper had 0pp at 2.10 R.E. where ? for 2 ????? ???? Orn 2.00-3.00 acres.	
	13		The first has been fairly quiet & trouble ????? to be ?????. Sketch ????? fairly active. Bombs dropped in E.85.A. — E ???? Type of ??????. we'd own ????? not our trench. A ??? shell was offered.	
	14		C. R. A. called. Very quiet — nothing to report. Brash Officer called from 2.F.D ?.? ? ??? with a view to taking over.	
	15		Very quiet. Regiment 2.F.B.? called in taking over.	

WAR DIARY
or
INTELLIGENCE SUMMARY.
(Erase heading not required.)

Army Form C. 2118.

Hour, Date, Place	Summary of Events and Information	Remarks and references to Appendices
Chateau la Haie		
16	Spr. Handed over Boys to Col. Southam. 283 Bde. Staff moved out - Balloon arrived on centre top staff of 290th Bde. he returned to HENU	
17	Nothing to report.	
18	Started class for junior Officers.	
19, 20, 21st	Nothing to report.	
22	Col Kennerigh appointed OC 4th R.A. R.F.A. - 15 Hundreds received	
23	Nothing to report	
24	Col. Kennerigh left to take on new command	
25 & 26	Nothing to report	
27	Col. E Pollaufer took on command of 253 Bde.	
28, 29, 30	Nothing to report.	Officer class ended
31	Brigade travelled to MEZEROLLES. Left PAS 7am. arrived 11.45am	
	GSO B5 had 2 staff cars on his march	

56th Divisional Artillery
(Right Group)

283rd BRIGADE R. F. A.

SEPTEMBER 1916.

… R.F.A.

WAR DIARY
or
INTELLIGENCE SUMMARY

Army Form C. 2118.

Place	Date	Hour	Summary of Events and Information	Remarks and references to Appendices
MEZEROLLES LE MEILLARD	Sept 1st	—	Left MEZEROLLES for LE MEILLARD.	
	2nd	—	2/Lt Gordon Pottinger joined Bde. from 97th Bde. 21st Divn. Battery question in LE MEILLARD very difficult – 3 Batteries to accomodate.	
	3rd	—	Left LE MEILLARD for CARDONETTE.	
LARDONETTE	4th	—	Left CARDONETTE for DAOURS. C/283 Battery moved up into action from DAOURS.	
DAOURS.	5th	—	Left DAOURS for Bivouacs near BRAY-sur-Somme.	
Nr BRAY-s-S	6th	—	Two guns of 93rd Battery attached to A/281 Batty, and two guns to C/281 Batty. 93rd Battery (split up as above) moved up into action.	
	7th	—	3 guns 104th Battery attached to C/280 Batty + one gun 109th attached A/281 Bty. 109th Battery (split up as above) moved up into action.	
	8th	—	Nothing to report	
	9th	—	Lt Col Pottinger appointed Liaison officer to 168th Inf. Bde.	
	10th	—	56th Divl Arty. Take over front from 6th Divl Arty	
	11th	—	Nothing to report	
	12th	—	Moved Wagon Lines to Bivouacs near MARICOURT	

Army Form C. 2118

WAR DIARY
or
INTELLIGENCE SUMMARY
(Erase heading not required.)

Place	Date	Hour	Summary of Events and Information	Remarks and references to Appendices
Near MARICOURT	13th	—	Nothing to report.	
"	14th	—	Major J.H. Borrodale appointed O/C Wagon Lines, 56th Div. Arty, & is attached to 283rd Bde. R.F.A. Lt. Col. appointed Liaison officer to 168 Inf. Bde.	
"	15th & 16th	—	Nothing to report beyond supplying of Ammn. to Batteries in the line	
"	21st	—	2nd Lt. T.H.C. Davis slightly wounded on 1/10 th (C/283)	
"	22nd	—	Lt. Col. E. Pottinger & Staff return from line.	
"	23rd	—	Nothing to report.	
"	24th	—	Lt. Col. E. Pottinger appointed Liaison officer to 95th Inf. Bde. Lt. Col. returns.	
"	25th	—	2/Lt. J. Bloomer killed in action (93rd Bty) 2/Lt. G.J. Palfrey wounded (C/283)	
"	26th	—	Nothing to report.	
"	27th	—	Lt. Col. Pottinger appointed returns from line. Enemy aeroplane bombs camp.	
"	28th	—	Lt. Col. appointed Liaison officer to 33rd Inf. Bde.	
"	29th	—	Major Tomlin (Arty) attached to 283rd Bde. R.F.A.	
"	30th	—	2/Lt. G. McL. Grant to evacuated sick to Hospital. Lt. Col. returns. Enemy aeroplane bombs Camp - No damage to 283rd Bde Lines.	

1st Oct. 1916

Lt. Col. Ad/C for 11 Ct. R.F.A.
Comdg. 283rd Bde. R.F.A.

100 95 / 2941 / 3

56TH DIVISION

DIVL TRENCH MORTAR BTYS
MAY 1917- JAN 1919

War Diary

Trench Mortar Batteries
56th Divisional Artillery

May - 1917 -

D.T.M.O.,
56TH DIVISIONAL
ARTILLERY.

Date 31·5·17.

WAR DIARY
or
INTELLIGENCE SUMMARY

Army Form C. 2118.

V SB } TRENCH MORTAR BATTERIES
X " } 56th DIVISIONAL ARTILLERY
Y " }
Z " }

MAY - 1917.

Place	Date	Hour	Summary of Events and Information	Remarks and references to Appendices
ACHIECOURT	1st MAY		Heavy & Medium Trench Mortar Batteries not in action owing to the General Artillery owing to the nature of the operations undertaken. It was not considered advisable to make the necessary preparation for H.T.M. ammunition & to maintain a supply of ammunition as the effect & accuracy was not established sufficient against the types of enemy trenches and entrenched dug outs opposite to the front line. The Reinforcement has been confined in interviewing & taking in hand by the advance of the Field Batteries in and obtaining the S.O.S. in the event of ammunition & enlarging the same from experimental battery positions.	
"	6th			
"	8th			
"	9 MAY	9 am	Inspection of Heavy & Medium Batteries with new armament & ammunition to obtain information by Commandant - School of Mortars 3rd Army.	
"	10 -		Road mending carried on throughout owing to the better weather.	
"	6th 27th		Daily training carried on including physical drill gun & drill musketry bomb throwing & route marching for all Officers men not employed in ammunition dumps in the forward area.	
S.2.d.30.15	28th		Orders received to relieve T.M. Batteries 57th Division Infantry Brigade at ACHIECOURT - Battle was clear of D.T.C. area at S.2.d.30.15 - Regt 5 T.B. S.V. 20 mm ACHIECOURT by 7pm on 28th Sect.	
S.2.d.10.15	29th 30th 31st		Section 3 Bivouac & making dug outs new T.M. School. V SB (Heavy T.M. Battery) left for 3rd Army T.M. School. Batteries had been mainly employed about 12 months ago as trained with a view to the W.O. School - as they received no permanent attachment - and were in places to refit, was Rem W.D. acting Officer Commanding T.M. Battery	

Qu...h
B...
D.T.M.O.
56th Division Artillery

Vol 2

War Diary.

56th Divisional Artillery, T.M. Batteries

June. 1917.

WAR DIARY
or
INTELLIGENCE SUMMARY

(Erase heading not required.)

Army Form C. 2118.

TRENCH MORTAR BATTERIES
56TH DIVISIONAL ARTILLERY
JUNE 1917.

V "56"
X " "
Y " "
Z " "

Place	Date	Hour	Summary of Events and Information	Remarks and references to Appendices
	JUNE		Trench Mortar Batteries of this Division were not in action during the month as nature of operations in hand rendered their employment impracticable.	
LIGNY ST. FLOCHEL	1-14		V Battery together with 2 officers and 13 men of Medium Battery at 3rd Army T.M. School re-training	
S.2.d.50.15	1-14		Remaining personnel of Medium Batteries carried on Training Programme. ~~to Training~~	
			X Battery with 5 men from Y Battery at 3rd Army T.M. School	
LIGNY ST. FLOCHEL	15-30		Heavy Battery with remaining personnel of Medium Batteries employed making Gun Emplacements and Cable Trench under orders from 21st & 60th Divisional Artillery.	
	15-30			

[signature]
for D.T.M.O. 56 D.A.

56th Divnl Artillery
Trench Mortar Batteries

War Diary July. 1917.

D.T.M.O.,
56TH DIVISIONAL
ARTILLERY.
No.
Date.

Sheet 1.

WAR DIARY
or
INTELLIGENCE SUMMARY.
(Erase heading not required.)

Army Form C. 2118.

1/56 H.T.M. Bty.
X/56 T.M Bty
Y/56 T.M Bty
Z/56 T.M Bty

July 1917.

Hour, Date, Place July 1917.		Summary of Events and Information	Remarks and references to Appendices
1st to 4th	BOIRY-LE-MONT S.2.d.50.15.	All T.M. Batteries, with exception of X/56 T.M.Bty & part of Y/56 T.M.Bty. which were at 3rd Army T.M School doing a second course of training, engaged daily in route marching, gun drill, marching drill.	
5th	- do -	Batteries proceeded to ACHIET-LE-GRAND and 2" Mortar Stores & Kits in motor lorries where they entrained to ABBEVILLE	
6th	ABBEVILLE	Arrived ABBEVILLE 1.30 am. Left 7.30 a.m.	
7th	PROVEN	Slept on PROVEN Station night 7/8th.	
8th	- do -	Proceeded by motor lorries to INTERNATIONAL CORNER near POPERINGHE and were attached to Guards Divisional Artillery	
9th	INTERNATIONAL CORNER	Party from Third Army T.M. School arrived.	
10th	- do -	Cleaned guns & stores.	
11th	- do -	Struck bivouac at INTERNATIONAL CORNER 9am. and proceeded to new camp nearer to front line at A.12.b.2.5. (BELGIUM & FRANCE Sheet 28 1/40,000)	
12th	A.12.b.2.5.	One Officer, Two gun detachments from Medium Batteries supplied to reinforce Guards & 29th Div. Arty. T.M. Batteries in action in positions on West side of CANAL de L'YSER immediately East of BOESINGHE. These detachments were relieved every three days.	

Sheet 2

WAR DIARY

INTELLIGENCE SUMMARY.

(Erase heading not required.)

Army Form C. 2118.

Y/56. H.T.M. Bty
X/56. T.M. Bty
Y/56. T.M. Bty
Z/56. T.M. Bty

July - 1917.

Hour, Date, Place July 1917		Summary of Events and Information	Remarks and references to Appendices
12th.	A.12.b.2.5	2nd Lieut S.S. FRANKLIN (19th London Regt.) attd Y/56 T.M.Bty wounded. 2 ORs. Killed. 2 ORs. wounded.	
13th.	"	2nd Lieut N.H KIMPTON Z/56.T.M. Bty. wounded - died of wounds later in day.	
15th.	"	Lt. A.R.C. CROOM-JOHNSON (280th Bde R.F.A.) Lieut. W. KING (281st Bde R.F.A.) 2/Lt R.A WEISS (54th DAC) arrived to re-inforce Batteries and posted X/56. Z/56 & Y/56 T.M.Btys respectively.	
17th.	"	2/Lt. B.J.A LAWLESS (1/12th London Regt.) attd Y/56 T.M.Bty. Killed. 2 ORs. wounded	See Summary of
18th.	"	2. ORs. Killed.	
19th.	"	Y/56 T.M.Bty. relieved Z/29 T.M Bty. in front line. Lt W.H. KING Z/56.T.M.Bty. wounded - remained at duty. 1 oR wounded.	Special Operations attached
20th.	"	Lieut H CRAMER Z/56. T.M. Bty wounded (gassed). 2/Lt E.L. WOODS (280th Bde R.F.A.) arrived & posted to Y/56 T.M. Bty.	
21st.	A.5.d.O.8.	All personnel not in the line moved to new camp at A.5.d.O.8 as old camp was continually shelled.	
24th.	"	D.T.M.O. 56th Div Arty. took over Command of Guards, 5th, 29th Div Arty TM Batteries from D.T.M.O Guards Div Arty, owing to latter being invalided sick.	

Sheet. 3.

WAR DIARY
INTELLIGENCE SUMMARY.
(Erase heading not required.)

1/5th H.T.M.Bty
X/56 T.M.Bty
Y/56 T.M.Bty   July 1917.
Z/56 T.M.Bty

Army Form C. 2118.

Instructions regarding War Diaries and Intelligence Summaries are contained in F.S. Regs., Part II. and the Staff Manual respectively. Title pages will be prepared in manuscript.

Hour, Date, Place July 1917		Summary of Events and Information	Remarks and references to Appendices
24th	A.5.d.0.8.	1. OR Killed 8 ORs wounded.	
25th	"	Z/56. T.M.Bty - withdrawn	
26th 11am	"	All available N.C.Os & men carrying ammunition.	
27th	"	Enemy evacuated front line system	See Summary of Special Operations (attached)
28th	"	Fatigue party of 2 Officers 50 NCOs & men constructed Artillery track (see attached Summary)	
29th	"	Lt. H. CRAMER rejoined Z/56 T.M.Bty from Hospital.	
31st	"	Fatigue parties - 2 of 1 Officer & 25 NCOs & men each. Constructed Artillery track (see attached summary)	

Clark Kerr
Captain R.A.
D.T.M.O.
56th Div. A. Arty.

56th Div Arty. Trench Mortar Batteries.

Summary of Special Operations from 15th to 31st July 1917.

The front which extended from B.5.d.8.7. to B.12.d.8.7. was divided into two Artillery Groups with about an equal extent of front, the 29th Div Arty being on the Right and Guards Div Arty on the Left.

On this front twenty four 2" Medium two 6" Medium and four 9.45" emplacements had been constructed. 8 Medium and 2 Heavy Mortars were in action in the Right Group and eight 2" two 6" + two Heavy T M s in Left Group. Their task was to destroy all the enemy's front-line defences, wire and trenches, and as much of their communication + support trenches as was within their range. This was effectively done as subsequent examination of the ground shewed that the enemy front line system, with the exception of a few strong concrete dug-outs and a few trenches on the extreme right of the Right Group had been practically obliterated.

During these operations which commenced on the 15th July 1917 —   326 rounds of 9.45" Ammunition
            400   "   " 6"   "
         4,500   "   " 2"   "

were fired.

This large amount of ammunition had to be got forward to the front line from the D.A.C. dump at BLUET FARM by means of light tramway running from BLUET FARM through B.11. central past North side of the CHATEAU, to BOESINGHE High Street. From thence it had to be carried to front line by means of Infantry and T.M personnel carrying parties. The tramway could only be used after dark as it was not sunk in a trench and was under enemy observation.

From B.11 onwards this tramway was continually shelled at night and from this point was practically destroyed. After the 19th its use was discontinued and ammunition was carried from B.11 central by BRIDGE STREET trench to front line.

All available personnel of the 56th Div Arty T.M.s were employed on this ammunition supply.

On the 27th the enemy evacuated front line system

(The)

The following morning a fatigue party of 2 Officers and 50 N.C.Os & men from 56th. Guards. & 29th Trench Mortars, under command of Capt H. L. MASON V/Guards H.T.M. Bty, proceeded to BOESINGHE to construct an Artillery track from MAIN STREET, BOESINGHE to the CANAL. The party encountered a heavy barrage in the above mentioned village & on C.T.s, which delayed commencement of work. The track was completed, except for filling in C.T.s crossed, by 10am & party returned to Camp.

On the morning of the 29th D.T.M.O 56th Div Arty & Capt A. L. WALLACE M.C. reconnoitred the ground for continuation of the track on East side of CANAL and selected exact site for Aerial Railway.

At Zero hour (3·50 am) on 31st July a party consisting of one Officer & 25 O.Rs from each Divisional Artillery T.M's, in charge of Capt H. L. MASON proceeded to BOESINGHE, repaired the track which had been much damaged by shell fire & filled in C.T.s which it crossed.

This party was relieved by a similar party, at Zero plus 6 hours, in charge of Capt A. L. WALLACE M.C. V/56 H.T.M Bty, who started at once to cut a way through the top of the CANAL bank & improvised means of crossing the canal with any material available, as the R.E.s were unable to erect the Aerial ropeway till some hours later.

By means of carrying parties in addition to the ropeway, when erected, the required ammunition was conveyed across the CANAL before dark. Lieut CROOM-JOHNSON relieving Capt A. L. WALLACE M.C. & above party at 6 pm working the ropeway with 20 men.

The casualties during the above operations were:-

Officers Killed 2 Wounded 3   O.Rs. Killed 5 Wounded 15.

All these casualties took place when engaged on ammunition supply, with the exception of 1 Officer wounded 1 OR killed & 3 O.Rs wounded.

Y/56 Heavy Trench Mortar Battery
X/56 Trench Mortar Battery — Army Form C. 2118.
Y/56   —   do
Z/56   —   do   — August 1917

WAR DIARY
or
INTELLIGENCE SUMMARY Z/56

(Erase heading not required.)

Place	Date 1917	Hour	Summary of Events and Information	Remarks and references to Appendices
A.5.d.0.8.	August 1st	15h/14R	Carrying parties & fatigue parties supplied to Guards D.A.	Vol 4
	6th	6R	Rejoined 56th Divn & moved into camp at G.23.a.9.1.	
G.23.d.9.1.	7th	7R	C.R.A. 56th Divn inspected the Battery	
	8th/13th 10th&25th		Battery carried out gun drill & general training — Special attention being given to Box Respirator drill.	
	9th	9R	D.T.M.O. took over from the 30th. D.A. — two 6" Newton T.M's; four 9.45" T.M's & also A.O.D. certificate for two 9.45" TMS (certified "beyond repair")	
	14th	14R	D.T.M.O. took over from the 23rd D.A — five 9.45" T.M.s (in old positions)	
	15th	15R	1 Officer & 60 Men sent to reinforce R/Pack Section 56th D.A.C.	
	18th	18R	The above party returned. Lt. W.A Kimpton & NCO's proceeded to 3rd. Army T.M School for course of instruction in 6" Newton Stokes.	
	24th	24h	Handed over all 6" Newton Stokes and 9.45" Mortars to 141st D.T.M.O.	
	26th	26R	30 O.Rs sent to 280th. Brigade RFA and 30 ORs to 281st Brigade RFA as reinforcements for the Battery.	
	31st		1. O.R. Z/56 T.M. Bty Killed in Action whilst attached to D/381st Bty.	

Claude Pimm
Captain R.A.
D.T.M.O.
56th Divisional Artillery

35807. W16879/M1879 500,000 3/17 R.T. (1074) Forms/W3091/3   Army Form W.3091.

Cover for Documents.

Vol 5

Nature of Enclosures.

War Diary

56th Divisional Artillery Trench Mortar Batteries.

September

1917.

Notes, or Letters written.

WAR DIARY

INTELLIGENCE SUMMARY

Army Form C. 2118.

V/56. HEAVY TRENCH MORTAR BATTERY.
X/56. TRENCH MORTAR BATTERY.
Y/56 - do - do
Z/56 - do - do

SEPTEMBER 1917

Place	Date Sept. 1917	Hour	Summary of Events and Information	Remarks and references to Appendices
OUDERDOM	1st.		Personnel attached to Field Batteries entrained for BAPAUME with the Batteries to which they were attached. Remainder cleaned up camp and packed stores ready for the move.	
	2nd.	1.30pm	Entrained at ESQUELBECQUES with 2" Mortar and stores, the 9.45" and 6" Mortars having been handed over to relieving Division. Motor Transport to station was furnished by Corps.	
BAPAUME	3rd.	8.30am	Arrived BAPAUME. Camp established at H.32.a.8.6.	
	4th.		Rested.	
	5th.		D.T.M.O. reconnoitred positions with D.T.M.O. 2nd Division.	
	6th.		D.T.M.O. reconnoitred positions with O's.C. Y/56 and X/56.	
	7th.		30 men who had been attached temporarily to Brigades rejoined at 12 noon. 56th. Div Arty Trench Mortar Batteries relieved 2nd Div Arty Trench Mortar Batteries in the line. Relief completed by 9.30 pm. Owing to the distance apart of the enemy and our front line systems and to the fact that they had only recently been established, the outgoing Division had no T.M's in action, but two mine emplacements, one for 9.45" and one for 6" Mortars were in course of construction.	
MORONIES	8th.		Work commenced on the two above mentioned emplacements	
	9th - 11th		Working parties of all available personnel Heavy & Medium Batteries, on Heavy T.M emplacement in LABRICOURT. Working in Thawn reliefs to keep work continuous.	
	12th.		Working parties as above. 30 men rejoined from Brigade at 6 pm.	
	13th.		Working parties as above. 2 Officers & 25 O.R.s sent to Third Army T.M school for course in 6" NEWTON-STOKES Mortar.	
	14th.		Working parties as above. D.T.M.O. & 2nd/Lt R.A.WEISS reconnoitred new position for 6" T.M. Position selected in Sunken Road D.20.d.8.4.	
	15th.		Working parties as above.	
	16th.		Work commenced on new 6" position at D.20.d.8.4. The necessary men for this work being drawn from party on Heavy emplacement.	

(Cont'd)

(Contd)

2.

WAR DIARY or INTELLIGENCE SUMMARY.

V/56 HEAVY TRENCH MORTAR BATTERY
X/56 TRENCH MORTAR BATTERY.
Y/56   do - do - do
Z/56   do - do - do

Army Form C. 2118.

SEPTEMBER 1917.

Place	Date	Hour	Summary of Events and Information	Remarks and references to Appendices
MORCHIES	17th		Working parties as above. D.T.M.O. and O.C. V/56. reconnoitred an alternative position for Heavy T.M. Position selected D.26.d. 40.45.	
	18th to 27th		Working parties as above.	
	25th 26th		D.T.M.O. + 2nd/Lieut R.A.WEISS. reconnoitred for new position for 6" T.M. on 25R + 26R Position selected at D.13.c.2.0.	
	28th		Working parties as above. 2 Officers + 25 ORs returned from 3rd Army T.M. School with their 6" Newton-Stokes Mortar.	
	29th		Work commenced on new 6" position at D.13.c.2.0.	
	30th		Working parties on all four positions. V/56 returned four 2" Mortars to Third Army Gun Park ALBERT in accordance with Army instructions.	

Claude Brown
Captain. R.F.A
D.T.M.O
56th Divnl. Artillery.

C O P Y.

D. A. G.,
G. H. Q., 3rd. Echelon.

A.A., & Q.M.G.
56th. Division.
A.Q.X. 541.

Reference your C.R., No.140/452 of 27/4/17.

1. March War Diaries for 56th. Divl. Train and 193rd. Machine Gun Company were sent you on 25/4/17 under my AQX 541.

2. All important operations etc. concerning heavy and medium Trench Mortar Batteries have been included in Divisional and Brigade Artillery War Diaries.

May I be informed, please, if these small Units are now required to keep a separate War Diary.

(Sgnd.) .... Major,
For Major General,
Commanding 56th. Division.

10/5/17.

2.

Headquarters,
56th. Division.

1. Now received.

2. A separate War Diary should be rendered by Divisional Trench Mortar Batteries (Heavy & Medium). The Brigade Trench Mortars (Light) should be amalgamated with the Brigade War Diary. This will apply to future Diaries, please.

G. H. Q.,
3rd. Echelon.
13th. May, 1917.

(Sgnd.) H.Yates,
Captain,
D. A. A. G.,
for D. A. G.

Army Form C. 2118.

WAR DIARY or INTELLIGENCE SUMMARY.

(Erase heading not required.)

V/56. H.T.M.Bty
X/56 T.M.Bty
Y/56 T.M.Bty.
Z/56. T.M.Bty.

OCTOBER 1917.

Vol 6

Place	Date	Hour	Summary of Events and Information	Remarks and references to Appendices
MORCHIES	1-5th		Work continued on H. positions as at end of last month.	
	6th		X/56. T.M.Bty attached to 12th Division.	
	8th & 9th		On the night of the 8/9th Y/56 T.M.Bty. was engaged in a special operation in co-operation with the Left Group 56th Divnl. Artillery, in support of a raiding party from the 168th 8/Mx Btn who carried out a raid on the Magpies Nest an enemy post D.13 central at 11pm. The battery had one 6" Mortar in action, in a trench emplacement at HARROGATE AVENUE, firing from zero hour to zero plus 7 mins to the Sunken road D.14.c.66. At zero plus 7 mins T.M's ceased firing & Artillery barrage lifted to enemy supports, the object being to lead the enemy to believe that the attack would be on this point (THE BIRDCAGE) & not the Magpies Nest. Y/56. were only able to fire 5 rounds in the time, as the back of the rear support straightened out slightly & jarred out of the eye on the gun barrel at every round, letting the gun down causing much delay & considerable risk in firing the piece. The range was approximately 1,300 yds.	
	13th		V/56. fired 6 rounds on enemy work D.16.c.5.2.	
	14th		Y/56 fired 10 rounds on enemy work D.16.c.5.2.	
	15th		V/56 fired 9 rounds with hollow charge on fortified crater D.15.b.55.70. X/56 rejoined from 12th Divn. Whilst attached to 12th Divn this battery took part in preparatory bombardment for a raid on a large scale E. of MONCHY, firing 400 rounds (2") The raid was very successful 70 prisoners being captured.	

Army Form C. 2118.

2. Contd.

WAR DIARY
or
INTELLIGENCE SUMMARY.
(Erase heading not required.)

Instructions regarding War Diaries and Intelligence Summaries are contained in F. S. Regs., Part II. and the Staff Manual respectively. Title pages will be prepared in manuscript.

Place	Date	Hour	Summary of Events and Information	Remarks and references to Appendices
	17th		2/5Z. sent their 2" mortars to 3rd Army Gun Park ALBERT, having been re-armed with 6" Newton Stokes Mortars.	Ref Map PRONVILLE Edn. 3c 1/10,000
	18th		1/5Z fired 11 rounds on Road & Trench junction D.15.b.55.70. 1/5Z fired 6 rounds on Trenches D.14.a. 55.55 to D.14.a. 50.40	
	19th		A special minor operation was arranged by the Left Group 56th Divl Artillery, an organised shoot of 18 hrs to 4·5 Hours Heavy, Medium, Light Trench Mortars, on French Syphon road junctions in area D.8.C.4.0. being carried out between 3.30pm & 4·8pm. The guns, howitzers & T.M's, with the exception of the Heavy T.M fired an Sharp bursts of 3 muns. at 3.30, 3·50, & 4·5pm. The Heavy T.M firing 10 rounds during this period. One 6" medium T.M was in action in this sector firing 36 rounds during the three periods of 3 muns. Considerable damage to Enemy's trench system was done.	
	24th		1/5Z fired 10 rounds on Strong Point D.8.C.1.1.	
	25th		15 men from D.A.C. attached to Medium batteries to assist in work on emplacement. 2 New 6" Emplacements having been started on at D.19.a. & D.19.b.	
	27th		1/5Z fired 10 rounds on Strong Point D.7.d. 3.9. – 1/5Z fired 3 rounds on Sunken road D.14.d 60.55	
	29th		1/5Z fired 9 rounds on Strong point D.14.a 40.85 – 1/5Z fired 50 rounds on D.14.c.77. Work on all emplacements was pushed on energetically during the month. 1 6" Emplacement in action considerably improved – The other 3 nearing completion – The 2 9·45 Emplacement both being ready to fire from.	

Maude Johnson Capt.
D.T.M.O.
56th Divl Arty.

WAR DIARY
INTELLIGENCE SUMMARY
(Erase heading not required.)

Army Form C. 2118.

X/56 Heavy Trench Mortar Battery
X/57 Trench Mortar Battery
Y/56
Y/57
Z/56 56th T.M. Bty.
Z/57

1917 NOVEMBER

Instructions regarding War Diaries and Intelligence Summaries are contained in F.S. Regs., Part II. and the Staff Manual respectively. Title pages will be prepared in manuscript.

Place	Date	Hour	Summary of Events and Information	Remarks and references to Appendices
MORCHIES	1st		X/56 T.M. Bty returned their 2" mortars to Third Army Gun Park, being now armed with 6" Newton-Stokes mortars.	
	2nd		All Batteries working on emplacements	
	3rd		- do -	
	4th		- do -	
			Y/56 H.T.M. Bty in action firing on enemy strong points. 50 infantry attached to Batteries for the purpose of carrying ammunition for 6" mortars, from forward dump to emplacements. This carrying party was found to be a good arrangement as every man soon learnt his way to pits & what had to be done, thus the inevitable confusion and delay which occurs with strange parties of infantry each night was avoided.	
	5/6		All Batteries working on emplacements	
	7th		- do -	
			All medium Batteries in action cutting wire at three points in the QUEANT - BIRDCAGE (D.14.c.4.d) in preparation for feint attack on this front, arranged for Z day at the time of the main attack.	
	8th		Y/56 T.M. Bty cutting wire and destroying enemy trenches in continuance of above scheme.	
			Y/57 H.T.M. Bty normal firing on enemy trenches and strong points.	
	9th		V/56, X/56, & Y/56. T.M. Batteries engaged as on 8.R.	
	10th		1 - 6"+5" Heavy (Long) Mortar taken over.	
	11th		V/56, Y/56, & Z/56. T.M. Batteries engaged as on 8.R.	
			V/57 + X/57 engaged as on 8.R.	

Army Form C. 2118.

WAR DIARY
INTELLIGENCE SUMMARY
(Erase heading not required.)

Continued.

1917 NOVEMBER

Place	Date	Hour	Summary of Events and Information	Remarks and references to Appendices
MORCHIES	12th		X/5L engaged as on 8.i.R.	
	13th		V/5L, X/5L + Z/5L engaged as on 8.i.R.	
	14th		V/5L, X/5L, Y/5L + Z/5L " " " "	
	15th		V/5L, X/5L + Y/5L engaged as on 8.i.R.	
	16th		Six 6" Mortar + 8 beds sent to 36th Division.	
	17th		X/5L + Z/5L engaged as on 8.i.R.	
	18th		Y/5L + X/5L " " " "	
	19th		V/5L, X/5L + Y/5L " " " "	
	20th		V/5L, Y/5L + Z/5L " " " "	
	21st		See Summary of Special Operations attached.	
	22nd		V/5L firing on Sunken Roads in QUEANT BIRDCAGE.	
	23rd		V/5L firing on C.T's to HINDENBURG Support Line.	
			See Summary of Special Operations attached.	
			1. G.45" received from 36th Division to replace the one from LAGNICOURT position.	
	24th		V/5L firing on junction of MELBOURNE TRENCH with HINDENBURG LINE D.16.a. 02.66. (FRANCE 57C NE (20000)) in cooperation with Left Group 5th Divnl. Artillery.	
			Y/5L + Z/5L firing on HINDENBURG front line trench QUEANT BIRDCAGE	
	25th		V/5L + X/5L engaged as on 24.i.R.	

Army Form C. 2118.

WAR DIARY
INTELLIGENCE SUMMARY.
(Erase heading not required.)

3 Continued

1917. NOVEMBER

Place	Date	Hour	Summary of Events and Information	Remarks and references to Appendices
MORCHIES	26th		3rd Division returned three 6" mortars & 2 heds. V/56 & X/56 engaged as on 24th. V/56 Engaged as on 24th.	
	27th/28th			
	29th/30th		3rd Division extended its right taking over the front of the 167th Infantry Brigade 56th Divn. All 56th Divnl Artillery T.M. Batteries remained in position and came under the tactical control of 3rd Divnl. Artillery	
	30th		V/56 engaged as on 24th.	

Roland Browne
Captain. R.F.A.
D.T.M.O.
56th Divnl Artillery.

SUMMARY OF SPECIAL OPERATIONS 20th & 23rd Nov. 1917.

From the 9th to the 19th of this month all 6-inch Medium Batteries were engaged daily in cutting wire and destroying enemy's trenches at several different points in the QUEANT BIRDCAGE D.14 (57.C., N.E., 1/20,000) in preparation for the feint attack on the 20th inst.

The wire appeared to be successfully cut at four separate places.

On the morning of the 20th Nov. when the main attack to the South was being launched V/56 Heavy T.M. Battery and X., Y. and Z/56 6-inch Medium T.M. Batteries co-operated with 18-pounders and 4.5" Hows. of the Left Group 56th Divisional Artillery in an intense bombardment of the QUEANT BIRDCAGE to simulate an attack in this direction.

Zero hour was at 6.20 a.m. which was just as it was beginning to get daylight. Dummy tanks and a line of dummy infantry had been put out in "No Man's Land" during the previous night in D.13.d.

From Zero to Zero plus 4 minutes Y/56 T.M. Battery fired at 5 rounds a minute on the MAGPIE'S NEST, D.13.a.90.30, which was the left flank of the 18-pounder smoke barrage.

From Zero plus 4 to Zero plus 8 all 6-inch Mortars opened rapid fire on the lower end of the QUEANT BIRDCAGE D.14.c. and d., lifting at zero plus 8 on to trenches in D.14.a & c. as far up the QUEANT BIRDCAGE as their range would permit, at the same time that the field guns lifted their barrage.

At Zero plus 15 minutes all Mortars and guns ceased fire.

The enemy put down a barrage in "No Man's Land" in front of the dummy infantry and tanks and also on our front line, and later on shelled X. and Y/56 T.M. Batteries' positions.

During the intense bombardment (11 minutes) V/56 Heavy T.M. Battery fired 11 rounds on the HINDENBURG Support Line at D.7.d.78.85 and D.8.c.55.25 from two Mortars.

The four 6-inch Medium Mortars, in action, fired 174 rounds during the same period.

On 23rd Nov. a similar feint attack was made on the same place in co-operation with the real attack further South by the 168th Infantry Brigade. Heavy and Medium T.M's co-operated with the atillery as before.

This time the enemy did not put down a barrage, but retaliated principally on T.M. emplacements.

WAR DIARY
or
INTELLIGENCE SUMMARY

(Erase heading not required.)

Army Form C. 2118

Y/56 Heavy Trench Mortar Battery
X/56 Trench Mortar Battery
1917
December

Place	Date	Hour	Summary of Events and Information	Remarks and references to Appendices
MONT HES	Dec 7 6 10		Normal. Retaliation firing on line this to DUMOUR BIRDCAGE (D.14.C. and E.) 57.C.M.E. Y/52 also fired by Medium Batteries and No marie C.T.S & MINDEN & BURG Supports, and by V/56 Medium T.M. Battery. Two 6" mortars placed in temporary emplacements at G.24.a.6.1 so T.M. Position, as others in position for NOS purposes.	
	11		56th Divisional Heavy T.M. Battery relieved by 2/56 H.A.T.M. Battery. Relief completed by 3 pm. Y/56 sent a mortar to FRÉ[M]ICOURT and has Extra that this night.	
	12	11:30am	56th H.A.T.M. Battery left FRÉMICOURT + now emplaced by mortar trains to ANZIN running 3 pm.	
	13 20		T.M. Batteries remained in rest at ANZIN	
ANZIN	21		Y/56 + Z/56 T.M. Batteries relieved Y/31 + Z/31 T.M. Batteries in the line in the BAPR + GAVRELLE Section respectively. Each taking over 4 6" T.M. 2/56 T.M. Battery left in reserve – Y/56 T.M. Battery entering over one 9.45"(long) Heavy T.M. not in action.	
	22 31		The personnel of 56 T.M. Batteries were employed in repairing, camouflaging and constructing new mortar Aspects. Constructing new Aspects for the mortars at CUPOLA FARM [?]	

G.G.C. Cohen
Captain
D.T.M. O.C. Artillery
56th Divisional Artillery

Vol 9

War Diary
56.H.D.A — 1 m B.
January 1918

… Army Form C. 2118.

V/5th. Heavy Trench Mortar Battery
X/57. Trench Mortar Battery
Y/57. Trench Mortar Battery
Z/57. Trench Mortar Battery

1918
JANUARY

WAR DIARY
or
INTELLIGENCE SUMMARY.

(Erase heading not required.)

Place	Date	Hour	Summary of Events and Information	Remarks and references to Appendices
ANZIN.	1st. 15th. 8th.	A.M.	All available T.M. personnel working on existing and new emplacements in OPPY and GAVRELLE sectors.	
"		A.M.	D.T.M.O. reconnoitred twelve defensive positions for 9" Trench Mortars, 100 to 200 yards in rear of front line in accordance with XIIIth Corps Scheme.	
"	6th.		Trench Mortar H.Qrs. mess billets at ANZIN evacuated and new H.Qrs. in CUPOLA CAMP G.H.Q. Central occupied.	
"	8th.		Medium Batteries in the line relieved by 62nd Divn Arty Trench Mortar Batteries - Relief completed by 4 p.m. Party in at billets at CUPOLA CAMP proceeded on the trails which brought the Kleine T.M. Batteries Nucleus at CAMBLIGNEUL. The Personnel relieved in the line proceeded to and spent the night at CUPOLA CAMP.	
CAMBLIGNEUL.	9th.		Party from the line proceeded by Lorry to CAMBLIGNEUL.	
"	10th.		Rested	
"	11th. 12th.		Kit Inspections by B.C.'s. Physical Exercises, Marching and Sitting up drill.	
"	13th.		Inspection of all Batteries, Stores by D.T.M.O.	
"	14th.		Physical Exercise, Marching etc.	
"	15th. To 31st.		All available personnel sent on working parties for the construction of horse standings for Divisional Artillery at A.C.R. CAUCOURT, PREVENT CAPELLE.	

Claude Rhone
Captn. R.F.A.
D.T.M.O. Artillery
56th Divisional Artillery

Instructions regarding War Diaries and Intelligence
Summaries are contained in F.S. Regs., Part II.
and the Staff Manual, respectively. Title pages
will be prepared in manuscript.

Army Form C. 2118.

51st Divisional Artillery
Trench Mortar Batteries

1918
Month February

WAR DIARY
INTELLIGENCE SUMMARY.
(Erase heading not required.)

VOL 10

Place	Date	Hour	Summary of Events and Information	Remarks and references to Appendices
CAMBLIGNEUL	1/8/12		All available personnel working on construction of CAUCOURT & FREVENTCAPELLE.	
	8th		Above parties returned to CAMBLIGNEUL.	
	9th		RE inspection etc by B.C.	
SIMCOE CAMP (near ROCLINCOURT)	10th		Adv Hd Qtrs 62nd D.A.T.M. Bs - HQrs at SIMCOE CAMP - 8"-6" Mortars in forward positions taken over. Relief of 62nd D.A.T.M. personnel in the line completed by 6pm.	
	11th		Rear party left at CAMBLIGNEUL relieved Rear party of 62nd D.A.T.M. Bs at SIMCOE CAMP. 9th to 11th 1889 torres med for Garrison by personal stores - The same lorries bring used by 62nd D.A.T.M. Bs	
	13th		Work commenced on forward positions for "A" "E" Mortars	
	17th		Batteries reorganised into 2 Medium Batteries of 6 Mortars each. D.T.M.O. reconnoitred positions in RED LINE in accordance with XIII Rs	
	21st		Orders & structures	
	27th		Work commenced on positions in RED LINE. Removed Mortar from forward positions close to OPPY WOOD as railways were impossible.	
			No firing done as positions required a lot of work to be done.	

C Craig Johns
Lieut RFA
DA TM O 51st Div Artillery

WAR DIARY

56th DIVISIONAL ARTILLERY TRENCH MORTAR BATTERIES.

M A R C H

1 9 1 8

Attached:-
Appendices 1, 2 & 3.

56th Divisional Artillery Trench Mortar Batteries

Vol II

WAR DIARY

MARCH 1918

Army Form C. 2118.

WAR DIARY

INTELLIGENCE SUMMARY

X/5L Trench Mortar Battery.
Y/5L Trench Mortar Battery.

MARCH 1918

Place	Date	Hour	Summary of Events and Information	Remarks and references to Appendices
SIMCOE CAMP MR. ROCLINCOURT	10/3/18		All available personnel of both Batteries employed working on three reserve positions on BAILLEUL WILLERVAL LINE (old Blue system).	
		6R.	X/5L Battery were cutting wire at C.13.c.50.15 and C.13.c.1.9 in preparation for raid by 168th Inf. Bde. Used 100 rounds.	See T.M. Report given No 12 appendices 1.
		7R.	X/5L Battery negotiated wire at C.13.c.1.9 successfully with aeroplane observation. 11 rounds fired. — Firing for effect on above target. 9am. 6" Newton Trench Mortars which received from Ordnance making dark batteries up to establishment.	
		8R.	X/5L Battery came as for 7th with the addition that hay fire 8 rounds on a hostile working party disposing it. — 188 rounds fired.	
		9R.	X/5L Battery fired 65 rounds on enemy trenches at C.13.c.55.15 and C.13.c.40.95 in support of raid by 168th Inf. Bde. The raid was successful — five prisoners being taken.	
		10R.	Working party of 10 other ranks from D.A.C. returned to their unit.	
		11R.	X/5L Battery fired 25 rounds on new work in enemy front line C.13.c 35.95. Y/5L " " 9 " " enemy wire at C.13.s.d. 3.5. reporting in preparation for raid by 169th Inf.try Bde.	
		12R.	Y/5L Battery fired 40 rounds on wire on 11R.	
		13R.	Y/5L " " 60 " " " 11R.	
			Y/5L " " 82 " " " 11R. 118 also on wire at C.25.c.25.00	
		14R.	Y/5L " " 15 " " " " " " Trouble was experienced with steel stopped to effect repairs.	

Army Form C. 2118.

WAR DIARY — Continued.

X/5L. Trench Mortar Battery
V/5L. Trench Mortar Battery

INTELLIGENCE SUMMARY.

(Erase heading not required.)

Instructions regarding War Diaries and Intelligence Summaries are contained in F.S. Regs., Part II. and the Staff Manual respectively. Title pages will be prepared in manuscript.

Place	Date	Hour	Summary of Events and Information	Remarks and references to Appendices
	16th		V/5L. Battery fired 6 rounds a.a. on 11h. One round fell short into our own front line, killing one man & wounding another. There was no explanation for this erratic round as the mortar and gunner was shooting well, books before and after the shot. V Battery did not co-operate and Divnl. Artillery so arranged. See statement under No. 23) (Appendix No. 2). As the infantry were always short shooting whilst a 2 on account of the short round during the afternoon. The shot was not successful.	
			16 R X/5L T.M. B.G. — wounded gas shell.	
	17th		13 OR. position in RED LINE.	
	18th		6 firing — 30 men from D.A.C. attached to V Battery as additional working party.	
	21st		V/5L. Battery by sound, on organised shell holes C.25.L.9.8. Hostile T.M. at C.2L.a.2.7. with good effect.	
	22nd		20 men from D.A.C. attached to V battery returned to their unit.	
	23rd		X/5L Battery fired 40 rounds on hostile T.M. at C.13.c 60.10	
			V/5L " " 21 " " organised shell holes C.25.L.9.8.	
	26/27		No firing.	
	27R		X/5L. Battery fired 81 rounds on enemy trenches C.13.c 60.20	
			" — 310 " " " " C.25 d 50.25 and C.25d 60.40	
			V/5L " " " " also C.25.L.9.8.	

— 3 — continued —

X/56 Trench Mortar Battery.
Y/56 Trench Mortar Battery

WAR DIARY

INTELLIGENCE SUMMARY.

Army Form C. 2118.

Place	Date	Hour	Summary of Events and Information	Remarks and references to Appendices
	28th/29th		See appendix No 3.	Appendix 3.
	30th		X/56 & Y/56 T.M Batteries relieved in the line by 4th Canadian Divisional Artillery Trench Mortars. 56th D.A.T.M Batteries moved out of SIMCOE CAMP to rest camp at ANZIN.	
ANZIN	31st		56th D.A T.M Batteries marched to ECOIVRES.	

From 1st to 27th of the month all T.M personnel, when not in the front line, were employed on construction of emplacements in front line on RED LINE systems.

The members availed for this work were, however, quite inadequate without outside assistance which was practically unobtainable owing to the amount of work to be done by all other units.

Claude Ekins
Captain R.F.A.
D.T.M.O. 56 Divisional Artillery.

A P P E N D I C E S

1, 2 and 3.

SECRET.

APPENDIX No. 1.

56th DIVISIONAL ARTILLERY TRENCH MORTAR OPERATION ORDER NO. 12.

T.M. CO-OPERATION IN RAID NEAR OPPY.

1. The 168th Infantry Brigade will raid the junction of COKE and FRESNOY TRENCHES at B.12.d.8.8. with the object of securing an identification.
   The hour and date of the raid will be notified later.

2. Preliminary Wire Cutting by T.M's.
   X/56 T.M.Bty. will cut wire at C.13.c.1.9. and C.13.c.40.15.
   This will be done with aeroplane observation.
   The cutting of the wire will be carried on for several days previous to the raid and will start on the morning of the 6th inst.
   The garrison of the posts will be responsible for keeping the gaps open at night.

   AMMUNITION EXPENDITURE - 100 rounds per day - unless otherwise ordered.

3. T.M. Programme during the Raid.
   X/56 T.M.Bty. will fire on enemy trenches immediately in rear of the gaps cut in the wire at C.13.c.25.95. and C.13.c.55.15. from Zero to Zero plus 20.

   AMMUNITION EXPENDITURE - 100 rounds per gun.

Copies to.
  X/56. T.M. Bty.
  168th Infty Bde.
  280th. Bde. R.F.A.

5.3.18.

O. Thomson
Major R.F.A.
for D.T.M.O.,
56th Divisional Artillery.

APPENDIX No. 2

SECRET.

APPENDIX T.M.4 to
56th DIVISIONAL ARTILLERY ORDER NO. 23.

1. **From Zero to Zero plus 5 minutes.**

    Y/56 T.M.Bty. will open intense fire on CRAWL TRENCH with one mortar from night position.

    From Zero plus 5 to Zero plus 45 minutes.

    On same target at slow rate.

    At Zero plus 45 minutes.

    Cease fire.

    Rates of fire.
    Intense — 5 rounds per minute.
    Slow   — 2   "   "   "

2. The Officer i/c Y/56 T.M.Bty. will synchronise his watch with that of O.C., Q.W.R., at Battalion H.Q., in the line.

3. Z day   - 18th.
   Zero hour - 10.0 P.M.

                                        Captain, R.F.A.
                                          D.T.M.O.,
                                    56th Divisional Artillery.

16.3.18.

APPENDIX No. 3.

6" MEDIUM TRENCH MORTAR REPORT
OF THE OPERATIONS OF THE 28th MARCH 1918.

On the night of 27th/28th March there were only five 6" Medium Trench Mortars in action, two in the front line system in BLUE ALLEY at B.24.b.30.55. and three in defensive positions behind the RED LINE, the personnel from the four mortars in the GAVRELLE Sector having been withdrawn that night as they had fired all their ammunition during the day preparatory to withdrawing all 6" mortars to the RED LINE in accordance with orders received.

These orders were cancelled later in the day and as on receipt of the "Counter" order the Section in BLUE ALLEY had 91 rounds left they remained in action. Their orders were to retaliate for any heavy T.M. bombardment of our front line, and in the event of an S.O.S. signal to open fire at rapid rate as long as the S.O.S. or ammunition lasted.

If it was found necessary to retire their orders were to disable their mortars and proceed down VISCOUNT STREET to Right Battalion Headquarters and there take orders from the Batt. Commander.

This Section consisted of one officer, Lieut W.B. FALCONER, and 9 O.R's. As no news of any kind has been received from them since the evening of the 27th it is surmised that they were surprised by the enemy whilst firing on their S.O.S. lines and were all killed or taken prisoner.

The four mortars in the GAVRELLE Sector were lost.

The three mortars behind the RED LINE were situated as follows:-

Two in rear of DITCH POST and one in rear of BAILLEUL EAST POST.

The emplacements were connected by wire to HOCKEY and TANK O.Ps, respectively, but unfortunately, communications to these O.Ps were cut early in the day. However, in accordance with instructions, the officers in charge at both positions kept in touch with the Infantry, though the only means of communication was by runner, or going personally over the open to the RED LINE.

Both officers kept a constant look-out during the attack on 28th, but did not fire as the enemy did not appear in the open within the limit of their range, and they received orders from the Infantry not to fire on THAMES & TYNE C.Ts as they had men in these trenches in advance of the RED LINE.

On the night of the 29th/30th, the mortars in rear of DITCH POST fired 52 rounds between 11.30 and 12.30 p.m. at request from Infantry to ward off a bombing attack down THAMES. The attack was successfully beaten off.

As there was not further request from the Right Infantry Brigade and no S.O.S. up to the time of being relieved on night of 30th, the officer at this position reserved the remainder of his ammunition for emergencies.

At the position in rear of BAILLEUL POST the mortar was in action on three occasions, twice in response to requests from the Left Infantry Brigade and once in response to an S.O.S. Signal. 80 rounds were fired during the S.O.S and 40 on the other two occasions.

Both positions were heavily shelled and had considerable trouble from gas.

The total casualties resulting from the operations were :-
    1 officer and 9 O.R. missing from the position in front system and
    1 O.R. killed and two wounded from positions in rear of BAILLEUL POST.

Claude Robinson
Captain, R.F.A.,
D.T.M.O.
56th Divl. Artillery.

30-3-18.

56th Divisional Artillery.

56th DIVISIONAL TRENCH MORTARS

APRIL 1918.

WAR DIARY or INTELLIGENCE SUMMARY

Army Form C. 2118.

X/5L Trench Mortar Battery
V/5L Trench Mortar Battery

April 1918

Place	Date	Hour	Summary of Events and Information	Remarks and references to Appendices
ECOIVRES	1st/2nd		Examining, cleaning and refitting all mortar stores and equipment.	
	3rd		As for 2nd - Gun drill and marching drill.	
	4th/8th		Physical drill; gun drill and gas drill. Signallers of both batteries given daily instructions in buzzing and care & repair of telephone lines by two N.C.O's from R.A. Signals attached to T.M. Batteries for this purpose.	
	9th		T.M. Battery marched to MONTENESCOURT, mortars and stores being transported by lorry. Received six 6" Newton Mortars to replace those lost on 28-3-18 – completing establishment.	
MONTENESCOURT	10th		Reconnaissance made by D.T.M.O. & B.C's for positions for defence of BLANGY TRENCH this being the second line of defence on the front taken over by 56 Division. Positions immediately North and South of SEAURAINS were selected.	
	11th		Two sections per Battery and three officers moved up to billets in RONVILLE CAVES and commenced work on the new positions.	
	12th/13th		Working on new positions.	
	14th		Working on new positions. By 6pm four mortars were in action and 200 rounds per mortar at the emplacements. The C.R.A. congratulated the Batteries on the amount of work done in so short a time. H.Q.s & details of T.M. Batteries moved to SIMENCOURT.	
SIMENCOURT	15th		Improving positions and constructing ammunition dug-outs. A fifth position was reconnoitred.	
	16th		Fifth position started – remainder as for 15th.	

Army Form C. 2118.

WAR DIARY *Continued*
INTELLIGENCE SUMMARY.
(Erase heading not required.)

APRIL 1918

Place	Date	Hour	Summary of Events and Information	Remarks and references to Appendices
SIMENCOURT	17R. 18R.		Fifth mortar in position with 100 rounds - remainder as for 15R.	
			A new emplacement for the mortar South of BEAURAINS at M.16.A. Started, 300 yards in advance of the old position. This alteration had to be made as BINGLEY TRENCH was advanced about 300 yards at this point. This mortar was moved into the new emplacement three days later.	
	19th/24		Improving and drawing positions and constructing ammunition dug-outs.	
	29R.		5th D.A. Trench Mortar Batteries relieved 15th D.A. T.M. Batteries taking over seven mortars in position in the new sector in exchange for seven mortars handed over at rest billets. The new sector taken over by 5th D. with Artillery from 15th D.A. extended the front held by former mortars to the main ARRAS - LENS Railway line.	
	30R.		Both batteries as for 29R/30R.	

Octave Pinan
Captain R.9.A.
D.T.M.O.
52nd Divisional Artillery

Army Form C. 2118.

X/56 Trench Mortar Battery
X/56 Trench Mortar Battery

9/X/3 MAY 1918

WAR DIARY
or
INTELLIGENCE SUMMARY.

(Erase heading not required.)

Instructions regarding War Diaries and Intelligence Summaries are contained in F.S. Regs., Part II. and the Staff Manual respectively. Title pages will be prepared in manuscript.

Place	Date	Hour	Summary of Events and Information	Remarks and references to Appendices
SIMENCOURT MAY 1918	1st/µ2.			
	4/3.		Building ammunition recesses. Constructing 4 new positions at — 2 East of ARRAS CEMETERY and 2 West of BEAURAINS. Improving emplacements and laying telephone lines - getting 300 rounds per mortar to the positions.	
	30h		2 ORs (X/56) wounded.	

31st May 1918.

Blanche Simmons
Captain R.F.A.
DTMO
56th Divnl Artillery

Army Form C. 2118.

WAR DIARY
or
INTELLIGENCE SUMMARY.

X/56. T.M. Bty.
Y/56 T.M Bty

VR 14 JUNE 1918

(Erase heading not required.)

Place	Date	Hour	Summary of Events and Information	Remarks and references to Appendices
SIMENCOURT	4th		Position at N7a.65.90. to cover front line reconnoitred.	
	6th		2 - 6" Mortars received on loan from First Army T.M. School.	
			Position at N.7a 65.90 commenced.	
	12d		" " " Complete + 1 mortar in action.	
	15th		Fired 10 rounds on N.8.a 77.55. & 18 rounds on N.2.c.73.2".	
	16.R.		" 7 " " " 7 rounds on N2c. 73.24 & not ground	
			on N.2.c. 73.15 & N.2.c. 73.35.	
	18.R.		Fired 10 rounds on N.8.a 72.63. 17 rounds on N.8.a. 72.20 & 13 rounds	
			on N.8.a. 83.20	
	27th.		Fired 40 rounds on N.8.a 37.87.	
			During the month the defensive positions have been improved.	
			During the month 40 men from D.A.C. were taken on 6"T.M.	
			by attachment for a period of 7 days, but no far being	
			at rest billets used for their training.	

Claude P. Amiss
Captain R.A.
D.T.M.O.
56 Divisional Art.

Army Form W.3091.

Cover for Documents.

Nature of Enclosures.

SECRET

Original War Diaries:-

H.Q. 56th Div. Arty,
280th Brigade, R.F.A,
281st Brigade, R.F.A
56th D.A.C.
X Y V/56 T.M. Batteries.

JULY 1918

Notes, or Letters written.

ORIGINAL

WAR DIARY or INTELLIGENCE SUMMARY

Army Form C. 2118.

1/56 Trench Mortar Battery
1/56 Trench Mortar Battery

July 1916

Place	Date July	Hour	Summary of Events and Information	Remarks and references to Appendices
SIMENCOURT	2nd	6/R	1/56. fired 5 rds on N.8.a.80.55 - 5 rds on N.2.c.65.35 and 15 rds on N.2.d.10.50	
		10/R	" " 10 rds " N.8.a.83.20 - 15 rds on N.2.b.51.20 " 15 rds " N.8.a.65.70.	
			" " 7 rds " N.8.a.80.25 and ranged on N.8.a.80.55	
	10.R		" " 15 rds " N.8.a.80.25 and 15 rds on N.8.a.70.50.	
	11.R		" " 20 rds " N.2.c.70.25 " 30 rds " N.8.a.90.03.	
	13.R			
	14.R		1/56 handed over 2 mortars in defensive positions G.30.a.68.73 and G.30.a.62.65 to 1/51.R.D.A. and for over 2 mortars not in action consequent on alteration of Northern Divnl. Boundary.	
	14.R		1/51 fired 20 rds on N.2.a.65.50 and 20 rds on N.2.a.10.50	
	14.R		" 10 rds " N.8.a.80.35 " 20 rds " N.8.c.70.97 and 10 rds on N.21.a.20.45	
	21st		Relieved by 1st Can D.A.T.M. Bde. - Relief completed by 4 pm	
AUBIGNY	22nd		Moved by lorry to AUBIGNY	
	23/30		Entrance training	
	30.R		D.T.M.O. made reconnaissance of SAVY O sub Sector G.H.Q. Line	
SIMENCOURT	31st		Moved to SIMENCOURT by lorry - preparatory to relieving 1st Can D.A.T.M. Bde.	

Frank Putnam
Captain R.A.
D.T.M.O.

578 TM 846
296
785 16

WAR DIARY
INTELLIGENCE SUMMARY.
(Erase heading not required.)

Army Form C. 2118.

X/56 Trench Mortar Battery.
a Y/56 Trench Mortar Battery.

AUGUST, 1918.

VOL 16

Place	Date AUGUST	Hour	Summary of Events and Information	Remarks and references to Appendices
SIMENCOURT.	1st		Relieved 1st Can. Div. Arty. Trench Mortar Bde. in the line. - Relief completed by 4 pm.	
do -	2nd to 16th		Constructing new emplacements in the Main Line of Resistance.	
- do -	17th		Relieved by 15th D.A. Trench Mortar Batteries. Personnel withdrawn from the line and resting at SIMENCOURT.	
- do -	18th		Mobile 6" Trench Mortar held at taken to First Army School of Mortars for trial.	
- do -	22nd		20 O.Rs. to BLAIRVILLE Dump as working party. 20 O.Rs. each to 280th Bde R.F.A and 281st Bde. R.F.A. constructing and repairing Artillery tracks.	
WAILLY.	26th		Non resting personnel moved to WAILLY.	
58.6.85.85	27th		Non resting personnel moved to 58.6.85.85.	

31-8-18.

Claude Rinnin
Capt. R.3.A.
D.T.M.O. 56th Div. Arty.

Army Form C. 2118.

WAR DIARY
or
INTELLIGENCE SUMMARY

X/56 Trench Mortar Battery.
Y/56 Trench Mortar Battery.

SEPTEMBER 1918.

(Erase heading not required.)

Instructions regarding War Diaries and Intelligence Summaries are contained in F.S. Regs., Part II. and the Staff Manual respectively. Title pages will be prepared in manuscript.

Place	Date	Hour	Summary of Events and Information	Remarks and references to Appendices
BOISLEAUX AU MONT.	1st to 5th		Twenty O.R. from each battery attached to 281st and 280th Bdes. R.F.A. for construction of artillery tracks and assisting Field batteries generally with emplacements etc. Remainder of T.M. personnel working on ammunition dumps.	
ARRAS.	6th 7th		All men from Bdes. and dumps returned to their units. 56th Div. Arty. T.M. Batteries moved to ST. SAUVEUR CAVES, ARRAS, and relieved 1st Div. Arty. T.M. Batteries.	
	8th to 17th		One Officer and 60 O.R. to 56th D.A.G. ammunition dump O.13.b.9.7. for work on dump.	
	18th/19th.		Divisional Boundary altered. The Division taking over more ground on their right from 3rd Canadian Division. 56th D.A. T.M. Batteries relieved 3rd Canadian T.M. Brigade, taking over 4 Mortars in action East of ECOURT ST. QUENTIN and RUMAUCOURT and 8 in reserve. All T.M. personnel with the exception of 15 O.R. withdrawn from Dumps.	
	20th.		T.M. personnel and Headquarters moved to SAUDEMONT 2	
SAUDEMONT	21st to 26th		All available personnel working on Emplacements and getting up sub-beds and T.M. Ammunition to the 6 Mortars which were being put in action for the operation commencing on 27th.	
	27th		See Appendix I - Special Operations attached.	
	28th		Batteries rested.	
	29th/30th		Withdrawing Mortars and sub-beds from emplacements to T.M. Headquarters. Cleaning up Mortars and equipment.	

Captain, R.F.A.
D.T.M.O., 56th Div., Arty.,

APPENDIX "I".

SPECIAL OPERATIONS. 27.9.18.

On the morning of 27th Sept. 1918, the 56th Division took part in the general attack on the enemy extending from the SENSEE RIVER to ST. QUENTIN.

The task of the 56th D.A.T.M.Batteries was to put an intense preliminary bombardment on the CANAL DU NORD from Q.23.a. to W.4.a.7.7. (Sheet 51.B. S.E.) including MILL COPSE and SAUCHY-CAUCHY Village, in preparation for the Infantry attack later in the day.

Y/56 T.M.Bty. had four mortars in action E. of RUMAUCOURT and X/56 Battery two E. of ECOURT ST. QUENTIN at an average distance of 800 yards from the CANAL.

This task was successfully carried out in spite of very heavy retaliation from machine-guns, minenwerfer and artillery of various calibre on these hastily constructed and very exposed positions of both batteries.

853 rounds were fired out of the 1,020 which were at the guns, the balance being unavailable as the component parts were destroyed by enemy shell fire during the bombardment.

Later in the day our Infantry took SAUCHY9CAUCHY with little opposition and few casualties.

At about 5.30 p.m., while the Infantry attack was in progress, 3 men of Y/56 T.M.Battery,(969965 Gnr. H.BARKER, 925976 Gnr. G.W.GIBBS, 5201 Gnr. H.SAUNDERS)having expended all their ammunition and being about to withdraw, were fired on by an enemy machine-gun from SAUCHY-CAUCHY. They,immediately, on their own initiative, rushed the machin-gun emplacement, capturing the gun and entire crew consisting of one officer,one sergeant-major and six other ranks.
This gun had been very active throughout the operations.

T.M. casualties were - killed - 2 O.R., wounded - 5 O.R., these were due to the fact that there had been no time to construct proper ammunition recesses for the amount of ammunition required and the men had to work very much in the open between the ammunition and the mortars.

Operation Orders and map attached.

Claude Robinson
Captain, R.F.A.
D.T.M.O.,
56th Divnl. Artillery.

30th September, 1918.

SECRET.

APPENDIX "T.M."
to
56th DIVISIONAL ARTILLERY OPERATION ORDER NO. 66.

(1) On a day (Z) and at an Hour (ZERO) to be notified later Nos. 1 to 6 Mortars in the line will be manned ready for action, Nos. 1, 2, 3 & 4 by Y/56 T. M. Bty., and Nos. 5 & 6 by X/56 T. M. Bty.

(2) From ZERO plus 10 mins. till Ammunition is expended.

TARGETS FOR DESTRUCTIVE SHOOTS.

Y/56 T. M. Bty. Nos. 5 & 6 guns.	MILL COPSE (200 rounds) MOULIN BRICHONBAULT, CANAL BANK (each side)
Y/56 T. M. Bty. Nos. 3 & 4 guns.	SAUCHY CAUCHY CHALK PIT, SAUCHY CAUCHY VILLAGE, CANAL BANK (each side)
Y/56 T.M. Bty. Nos. 1 & 2 guns.	RAILWAY JUNCTION (W.4.b.3.7.) CANAL BANKS (either side)

(3) **RATE OF FIRE.**

Not more than three rounds per minute.

(4) **AMMUNITION**

200 rounds per gun.   Fuze - Instantaneous.

(5) **RESTRICTIONS**

(a) Nos. 1 & 2 guns must not fire SOUTH of a line 500 yards NORTH of RAILWAY A. B. and parallel to it after ZERO plus 300 mins.

(b) Nos. 1 & 2 guns must not fire SOUTH of RAILWAY A.B. at all, except that the junction at W.4.b.3.7. may be engaged till ZERO plus 200 mins., BUT NOT AFTER.

(c) All guns stop by ZERO plus 840 mins.

NOTE.

Artillery barrage at ZERO comes down on the line 300 yards WEST of CANAL returning again at about ZERO plus 500 mins.

As there is a very large margin of time between ZERO plus 10 and ZERO plus 840 for expenditure of ammunition available favourable opportunities for firing and resting may be employed.

When ammunition is expended detachments will take cover or withdraw to Trench Mortar Headquarters at discretion of Section Commanders.

(6) ACKNOWLEDGE.

Claude Robinson
Captain, R.F.A.,
D.T.M.O.,
56th Divisional Artillery.

26. 9. '18.

Copies to:-
168th Infantry Brigade,
56th Div. Arty.,
War Diary,
X/56 T. M. Battery (3),
Y/56 T. M. Battery (3).

Army Form C. 2118.

X/56 Trench Mortar Battery.
Y/56 Trench Mortar Battery.

WAR DIARY
or
INTELLIGENCE SUMMARY.

(Erase heading not required.)

OCTOBER. 1918.

Instructions regarding War Diaries and Intelligence Summaries are contained in F. S. Regs., Part II. and the Staff Manual respectively. Title pages will be prepared in manuscript.

Place	Date	Hour	Summary of Events and Information	Remarks and references to Appendices
SAUDEMONT.	1st/14th		Not in action - Training.	
	15th		2 Mobile Trucks for 6" T.M. received.	
	17th		Came under command of C.R.A., 4th Can. D.A. consequent on 56th Divn. being relieved by 4th Can Divn.	
ESCADOEUVRES	22nd		Moved to ESCADOEUVRES - rejoined 56th Divn.	
	23rd/28th		Training.	
	29th		Satisfactory trial of Mobile T.M. - 40 rounds fired.	
	30th/31st		Training.	

31.11.18.

Claude Rhum
Captain, R.F.A.
D.T.M.O.,
56th Divisional Artillery.

Army Form C. 2118.

WAR DIARY
or
INTELLIGENCE SUMMARY.

X/56 Trench Mortar Battery.
Y/56 Trench Mortar Battery.

NOVEMBER 1918

Vol 19

(Erase heading not required.)

Instructions regarding War Diaries and Intelligence Summaries are contained in F. S. Regs., Part II. and the Staff Manual respectively. Title pages will be prepared in manuscript.

Place	Date	Hour	Summary of Events and Information	Remarks and references to Appendices
ESCAUDOEUVRES	3rd		Working party attached to 56th A.R.P.	
	4th		X/56 T.M.Bty attached to 280th Bde. R.F.A. and Y/56 T.M.Bty. attached to 281st Bde. R.F.A.	
	11th		Cessation of hostilities - Armistice signed.	
ONNEZIES	15th		Both batteries detached from the artillery Bdes. and moved to ONNEZIES. Move completed by 12.00.	
	19th/30th		Physical exercise, marching drill, rifle drill, practice in guard mounting etc.	
	23rd		All gun-stores, Guns etc. handed into D.A.D.O.S.	

30.11.18.

[signature]
Captain, R.F.A.
D.T.M.O.,
56th Divisional Artillery.

WAR DIARY

INTELLIGENCE SUMMARY

Place	Date	Hour	Summary of Events and Information	Remarks and references to Appendices
ONNEZIES	1 Dec	9am	X + Y & T.M. Baldwin moved to CIPLY	
	2 Dec		Baldwin engaged in Drill & Training in the mornings and attending Educational classes the men having the afternoons to themselves to prepare & pack ammunition	
	to			
	31 Dec			

Clarke Brown
Capt
D.T.M.O.
15th Divisional Artillery

Army Form C. 2118.

WAR DIARY
or
INTELLIGENCE SUMMARY.
(Erase heading not required.)

1/5th TM Bty
1/5 TM Bty

January 1919

Vol 1

Place	Date	Hour	Summary of Events and Information	Remarks and references to Appendices
CIPLY	Jan 1st to 31st		Batteries engaged on Drill and Training in the mornings and attending Educational Classes. The men having the afternoons to themselves not to attend or other amusements. A large number of men demobilized through march — a few months have been successful while on leave.	

31st January 1919

Blank Plumer
Cosham R.S.A
D.T.M.O
5th Div Arty

WO 95/29441/4

56TH DIVISION

56TH DIVL AMMN COLUMN
FEB 1916-MAY 1919

56TH DIVISION

War Diary
56th D.A.C.
Late 10th DAC

Feb
Vol. 5

WAR DIARY or INTELLIGENCE SUMMARY

Army Form C. 2118

10th DIV. AMM. COL. R.F.A.

Place	Date	Hour	Summary of Events and Information	Remarks and references to Appendices
LESPESSES	17.2.16		Section No 1 & 2 returned from NESDIGNEUL	
	17.2.16		2/Lt. J.S. Stoner promoted lieut during his absence. Capt P.W. Griffith promoted Temp-Major — appointment as adjutant.	
	21.2.16		Howitzer portion opened to column from ANNEZIN.	
	22.2.16		The column left LESPESSES to join the 56th DIV. in the SOMME district and the trainloads were made up as follows—	
	25.2.16		Five trains were required. 1st Train HQ + 1/3 Sec 1. 2nd Train 1/3 of Sec 1. 3rd Train 1/3 of Sec 2. 4th Train 1/3 Sec 2. 5th Train 1/3 Sec 3. 1/3 Sec 3. The first two trainloads entrained at BERGUETTE & these train loads at the station were extremely difficult owing to frost & snow the roads being extremely dangerous travelling. It must have been even the so— The first described detachment left LESPESSES at 12·30 p.m. 25/2/16 and the last detachment at 7·30 p.m. 25/2/16. The column arrived at PONTRENY at 1st at 8 A.M. 26/2/16 & the last at 7 A.M. 27/1/16 — The detraining had to be carried out by means of ramps — as the train loads arrived & detrained billets were occupied at ERONDELLE.	
ERONDELLE	26/2/16			

Army Form C. 2118

18th DIV. AMN. COL. R.F.A.

WAR DIARY
or
INTELLIGENCE SUMMARY
(Erase heading not required.)

Instructions regarding War Diaries and Intelligence Summaries are contained in F.S. Regs., Part II. and the Staff Manual respectively. Title Pages will be prepared in manuscript.

Place	Date	Hour	Summary of Events and Information	Remarks and references to Appendices
BRONDELLE	24/2/16		The column left here for ST LEGER via FLIXECOURT & ST OUEN travelling. The column left at 9-30 A.M. and arrived complete at 3-30 P.M.	
ST LEGER	27/2/16		The column on arrival billeted in the portion of the village north of the railway.	

P.W. Griffith
Major
o/c 18th D.A.C.
(late 18th DAC)

War Diary February 1916
56th Div. Amm Col.
R.F.A.
Vol VI

Army Form C. 2118

WAR DIARY
or
INTELLIGENCE SUMMARY
(Erase heading not required.)

56th DIV. AMN. COL. R.F.A.

Place	Date	Hour	Summary of Events and Information	Remarks and references to Appendices
ST. LEGER	4.3.16		CRA inspected the column in F.S.M.O.	
"	9.3.16		Army Chaplain 4th Class A. L. WATT. was attached to column.	
"	12.3.16		The column left ST LEGER at 7-45AM for HEM arriving there at 11-45AM. Sections 1 + 2 were billeted at HEM. Section 3 at HARDINVAL	
HEM	15.3.16		The column left HEM for ETRE-WAMIN at 8 A.M. arrived at 2-15 p.m. The whole column Billeted at ETRE-WAMIN.	
			"Extract from letter from Major Gen. C. HULL Comdg 56th Div- In connection with the hard of the division on the 12th from the DOMART to DOULLENS are the following were put in regards stern restraint of Div. Amm. Col.—	
ETRE-WAMIN	17/3/16		General Turn out— 2nd Lt. R.T.E. MASSEY 3/1/2 London F.A.B. attached for duty with column.	
"	23/3/16		Lt + Adj. J.S. STORRAR went to Westland on short leave.	
"	31.3.16		The horses of the column were inspected by the C.R.A. + to D.D.V.S. 3rd Army.	

J.W. Forfit Major
O/C 56th Div. Amm. Col.

Vol VII

War Diary
56 Div Am Col. R.F.A.
for APRIL 1916

WAR DIARY
or
INTELLIGENCE SUMMARY

(Erase heading not required.)

Army Form C. 2118

APRIL 1916   56th Div: Ammn. Column

Place	Date	Hour	Summary of Events and Information	Remarks and references to Appendices
ETREE - WAMIN	5-4-16		2nd Lt. LYNAM. J. E. left the column for attachment to the 1/3rd London Bde: R.F.A. to undergo Instruction.	
In Billets	16/4/16		2nd Lt. BOYDEN. P. joined for duty with the column.	
	29/4/16		General HEDLAM. J. Artillery advisor to G.H.Q. visited the column and inspected the lines.	

Bree Capt R.G.A.
OC 56th Div. Ammn. Col.

War Diary

50th Div. Amm. Col.
R.F.A.

WAR DIARY
or
INTELLIGENCE SUMMARY

(Erase heading not required.)

56 Div Amm Col RFA

Army Form C. 2118

Place	Date	Hour	Summary of Events and Information	Remarks and references to Appendices
ETREE WAMIN	8.5.16	7-15	DAC left ETREE-WAMIN en route for MONDICOURT arrived here at 11-15 A.M.	
MONDICOURT	15.5.16		Inspection of horses of 56th DAC by Lt. Gen. Sir T.D.O.SNOW KCB. G.O.C. 7 Corps.	
"	16.5.16		Lieut. V. STRANDERS. left for ENGLAND -	
"	17.5.16	12 Noon	The 280, 281st 282nd 283rd BACs were taken over to commence the reorganising of the Column on the new establishment in accordance with GHQ Letter No OB 818 -	
"	17.5.16		2/Lieut A.M. SPIERS. took over charge of the ammunition dump at HENU.	
"	20.5.16		Lieut A.H. MOEEING o/c late 283rd B.A.C. assumed command of No 3 Section.	
"	20.5.16		Capt W. BIRD. RFA. assumed command of B ECHELON. 56th DAC.	
"	27.5.16		The Reorganisation of 56. DAC Completed and the details of BAC marched off to the advanced base at ABBEVILLE under Capt. TALBOT. R.F.A.	

S L Griffiths Major. RFA
O/C 56 Div Am Col -

No 9

War Diary.
for Month of June 1916.
56 D'ole. R.Y.A.

Army Form C. 2118

WAR DIARY
or
INTELLIGENCE SUMMARY
(Erase heading not required.)

56 Div. Am. Col. R.F.A.

Instructions regarding War Diaries and Intelligence Summaries are contained in F.S. Regs., Part II. and the Staff Manual respectively. Title Pages will be prepared in manuscript.

Place	Date	Hour	Summary of Events and Information	Remarks and references to Appendices
MONDICOURT	13.6.16		Commenced taking up ammunition for the batteries. All ammunition issued out to two each night up to morning of 19/6/16 —	
	14.6.16	11 pm	Clerks arrived, hour —	
	15.6.16	12 noon	H.Q. with sections 1, 2 & 3 moved to PAS. HUTS. B echelon moved to Chateau HUTS at HENU	
HENU	21.6.16	noon	H.Q. & Sections 1 & 2 & 3 moved to chateau Huts at HENU. B echelon moved from Chateau HUTS to PAS. HUTS	
	24.6.16		Hostile aeroplanes dropped bombs on PAS. HUTS. no damage was done —	
	25.6.16		One man killed & 5 wounded (since dead) Attached 2D." Brigade in SAILLY.	
	26.6.16		Capt. B. BIRD 3/c B echelon took over command of 1/2 D.O. Battery	
	26.6.16		Lt. W.S. WATER assumed 2nd command of R. Peters vice Colt. the BIRD	
	27.6.16		37 (other ranks) joined unit.	
	28.6.16		Sergt WATER (wounded) to hospital.	
	29.6.16		42 other ranks arrived for T.M. Battery	
	30.6.16		2/Lt GEE slightly wounded remained at duty. 2/Lt R. PEW returned from hospital.	
			On Major B. Petrolly returned.	Histofte Regenbaye SSE DAC

Ke 10

War Diary.
July 1916.

56. Div. Amm. Col. R.F.A.

(ORIGINAL)

Army Form C. 2118

WAR DIARY
or
INTELLIGENCE SUMMARY
(Erase heading not required.)

July 1916
56 DIV. AMM. COL. R.F.A.

Place	Date	Hour	Summary of Events and Information	Remarks and references to Appendices
HENU	5-7-16		Casualty 1 O.R. wounded.	
"	7-7-16		2/Lt. S.W. MILLS, 2/Lt. P.A. HARRISON & 2/Lt. P.S. HOODLESS, joined the column.	
"	9-7-16		Lieut. M.J. SMITH & Lieut. A.H. MOREING were permitted by G.O.C. to assume the badges & rank of captain.	
"	10-7-16		Lieut. F.S. WELDON TAYLOR joined the Column.	
"	11-7-16		2/Lt. P.S. HOODLESS proceeded to join Y 56 Trench Mortar Battery. 2/Lt FENNELL posted to 282 Bde.	
"	12-7-16		Capt W.L.W. BIRD resumed command of B. Echelon	
"	14-7-16		2/Lt. S.W. MILLS Posted to 282 Bde R.F.A.	
"	15-7-16		2/Lt. J.W.D. FISHER Posted to 282 Bde. R.F.A. 2/Lt. J. BLUMER posted to 283rd Bde. R.F.A.	
"	17-7-16		2/Lt. R.St. JOHN CARR joined the 6 column	
"	18-7-16		2/Lt. H. KENNINGTON posted for duty to Artillery School 3rd Army.	
"	22-7-16		Lieut General Sir T. D'O. SNOW Comdg VII Corps inspected the horses of the Column, & expressed himself quite satisfied.	
"	25-7-16		2/Lt. H.W. ADAMS Posted to 282 Bde. R.F.A	
			Extract from London Gazette:-
			To be Temp. Lieut Colonel, Temp Major E.W. Griffith R.Y.A. Feb. 1916

Griffith
Lt Col
RFA OC DAC.

Original

Vol XI

War Diary
56 D.A.C. R.F.A.

1-8-16 — 31-8-16

Original

WAR DIARY
or
INTELLIGENCE SUMMARY
(Erase heading not required.)

Army Form C. 2118

AUGUST. 1916

56. DIV. AMM. COL. R.F.A.

Place	Date	Hour	Summary of Events and Information	Remarks and references to Appendices
HENU	1-8-16		1-8-16 to 30-8-16 In hutments at HENU. (A.Echelon).	
HENU	11-8-16		1-8-16 to 31-8-16 " " PAS. (B.Echelon).	
			2Lt. R.P. REW. posted to 283rd Bde R.F.A.	
			2Lt. P. BOYDEN. left for CALAIS.	
"	14-8-16		2Lt. A. McL. SPIERS posted to V/56. T.M.B.	
"	14-8-16		16 G.S. wagons (surplus to Establishment) dispatched by rail to BASE	
"	30-8-16		A.Echelon left HENU 10 A.M. Arrived at MEZEROLLES at 3 p.m. The 3 sections were billeted in the village for the night.	
MEZEROLLES	31-8-16		A.Echelon left MEZEROLLES at 9A.M. and arrived at GENNE - IVERGNY at 12.45 A.M. The 3 sections took up billets in the village.	
			B.Echelon, with 4 Trench Mortar Batteries, X56, Y56, Z56, & V56, attached, left PAS HUTS, and proceeded to OCCOCHES and took up billets for the night en route for GENNE - IVERGNY.	

96 [signature] Lt. Col. R.F.A.
Comdg. 56. Div. Am. Col.

56th Divisional Artillery.

56th DIVISIONAL AMMUNITION COLUMN R.F.A.

SEPTEMBER 1916.

Army Form C. 2118

WAR DIARY
or
INTELLIGENCE SUMMARY
(Erase heading not required.)

September 1916.
56 Div. Amm. Col. R.F.A.

Place	Date	Hour	Summary of Events and Information	Remarks and references to Appendices
GENNE-IVERGNY.	1-9-16		A Echelon at GENNE-IVERGNY. B Echelon at OCCOCHES.	
	3-9-16		A Echelon left GENNE-IVERGNY at 4.30 pm and arrived at BOIS BERGUE S at 8.45 pm. B Echelon with 4 T.M.B.s (x 56, y 56, z 56 and v 56 T.M.B.) left OCCOCHES at 3.15 pm and arrived at BOIS BERGUES at 4.30 pm.	
BOIS BERGU ES.	3-9-16		B Both Echelons with 4 T.M.B.s left BOIS BERGUES at 9 AM and arrived at VILLERS-BOCAGE at 5 pm.	
VILLERS-BOCAGE.	4-9-16		Both Echelons with 4 T.M.B.s left VILLERS-BOCAGE at 10.15 AM and arrived at DAOURS at 4.30 pm.	
DAOURS.	6-9-16		Left DAOURS at 8.45 A.M. A Echelon arrived at MAP. REF. 62D F25.b.8.2. at 12.50 pm. B Echelon at MAP. REF. E16.2 4.8. at 2.15 pm. (Joined XIV Corps), 2⁄Lt Bartine to Hospital.	
62 D. F25 b.8.2.	7-9-16		Commenced taking up ammunition and continued during the whole of the remainder of the month.	
	10-9-16		A Echelon left F 25 b.8.2. at 10 AM. and arrived at F29 b.7.7. 1.20 pm. B Echelon left E.16.2 4.8 at 9 AM and arrived at F25 b.8.2. 10.30 A.M.	
F 29 b.7.7.	12-9-16		5 men wounded and 4 horses killed while taking up ammunition.	
	13-9-16		Lieut. R.T.E. MASSEY to Hospital.	
	21-9-16		Capt BIRD. L.W.L. (OC B Echelon) assumed command of A Batty. 280. Bde. R.F.A. Lieut. WATSON. W.S. Assumed command of B Echelon.	
	23-9-16		Capt. E.C. GEE to Hospital.	
	26-9-16		Capt. E.C.G.EE returned from Hospital.	
	27-9-16		Bombs from Hostile air craft dropped in vicinity of camp.	
	28-9-16		Lieut. L.W.GEE admitted to Hospital	

E.W. Griffith Lt Col RFA
o/c 56 Div Am Col

Vol 14

War Diary
56 D.A.C.
NOVEMBER
1916

ORIGINAL

Army Form C. 2118

WAR DIARY
or
INTELLIGENCE SUMMARY
(Erase heading not required.)

NOVEMBER 1916.

56 DIV. AMM. COLUMN R.F.A.

Place	Date	Hour	Summary of Events and Information	Remarks and references to Appendices
F17 C.6.8.	1-11-16		Left F17.C.6.8. at 8 A.M. arrived at DAOURS at 5.15 p.m.	
DAOURS	2-11-16		Left DAOURS at 9 A.M. arrived at VILLERS BOCAGE 2.30 p.m. Lieut W.H. CARTER joined Column	
VILLERS-BOCAGE	3-11-16		Left VILLERS BOCAGE 9.30 A.M. arrived ORVILLE at 4 P.M.	
ORVILLE	4-11-16		Left ORVILLE at 8.45 A.M. arrived at ETREE-WAMIN at 2 P.M.	
ETREE-WAMIN	5-11-16		Left ETREE-WAMIN at 9 A.M. arrived at FREVIN-CAPELLE at 2-30 p.m.	
FREVIN-CAPELLE	8-11-16		2Lt. W.H. DEASON and 2Lt. R.T. KEENAN joined the Column.	
"	13-11-16		2Lt. L.W. BEE returned from sick leave. 2Lt E. BARTON who entered hospital on 6-9-16, struck off Strength having been evacuated to England on 25-10-16.	
"	14-11-16		The M.G.R.A. inspected the Column.	
"	16-11-16		2Lt G.C.H. DAY joined the Column.	

E.G.?, Capt.
?, Lt-Colonel, R.F.A.
Commanding th Divisional Ammunition Column

Vol 15

War Diary
56 D.A.C. R.F.A.

December 1916

(ORIGINAL)

WAR DIARY or INTELLIGENCE SUMMARY

Army Form C. 2118

56 DIV. AMM. COL. R.F.A.

DECEMBER

ORIGINAL

Place	Date	Hour	Summary of Events and Information	Remarks and references to Appendices
FREVIN CAPELLE	1-12-16		The Column at FREVIN - CAPELLE.	
CAPELLE	2-12-16		Left FREVIN - CAPELLE at 10 AM arrived AUCHEL at 5-30 P.M.	
AUCHEL	3-12-16		Left AUCHEL at 9 AM, arrived HAVERSKERQUE 3.30 P.M.	
HAVERS-KERQUE	6-12-16		Left HAVERSKERQUE at 10 AM, and took over billets at:- Hd Qrs. L.26 b.1.2. See.1. R 11 Central, See. No 2 L.24 c.2.7. See. No 3, L.26 a 2.8., See No 4 L.36 a 8.2. Map Reference. 36 A.	
			Lieut R.T.E. MASSEY rejoined the Column.	
L.26 b.12.	13-12-16		Capt F.J.HUNT R.A.M.C. M.O. ¾c Proceeded to 32nd C.C.S. for duty, Capt J Mc A. SCOTT RAMC, arrived, and took up the duties of M.O. ¾c. Column.	
L.26 b.12	16-12-16		2Lt. W.H. DEASON y 2Lt. R.T. KENNAN attached to D/282 Batty for instruction. 2Lt G.W. DAY attached to C/280 for instruction.	
			Lieut A.V. HEAL joined the Column.	
L.26 b.1.2	21-12-16		2Lt. J.T. CAPRON } attached to 56th Div. Arty School of instruction. 2Lt. L.W. GEE }	
L.26 b.12	26-12-16		D.D.V.S. First Army inspected animals of the column.	
L.26 b.12	27-12-16		36 (other Ranks) arrived from No 50 Base Depot. Capt. A. Adams. A.V.C. to 2/3 London Field Ambulance.	
L.26 b.12	28-12-16		Capt A. ADAMS. A.V.C. evacuated to No 7 C. C. S.	

E. C. C. Capt R.F.A.
for Lieut Col R.F.A.
Comdg. 56th Div. Amm.

Vol 16

War Diary
for January 1917

56 DAC

WAR DIARY
or
INTELLIGENCE SUMMARY
(Erase heading not required.)

Army Form C. 2118

56. DIV. AMM. COL. R.F.A.

JANUARY, 1917

Place	Date	Hour	Summary of Events and Information	Remarks and references to Appendices
As shown	2-1-17		Position of the Sections of the 56 D.A.C. on 1-1-17. Head. Qrs. L.26.b.1.2. No 1 Section R.11 Central No 2 " L.27.c.2.4. No 3 " L.26.d.2.8. No 4 " L.36.a.8.2. 4 How wagons with limbers, 12 drivers, & 24 horses, transferred from A/282 to No 1 Section. 4 G.S. wagons, 12 drivers, & 24 horses transferred to B.2 Echelon from A/282. These were transferred to complete to new establishment. The Div. Artillery now having 16 Howitzers.	
As shown	20-1-17		Capt. A. ADAMS. A.V.C. rejoined from field Ambulance.	
As shown	23-1-17		Lieut A.V. HEAL. attached to 281 Bde. R.F.A.	
As shown	24-1-17		Reorganisation of the D.A.C. The late No 3 Section became No 2 Section. The late No 2 Section became the 282 nd Army, field Artillery Brigade Ammunition Column. The D.A.C. now consisting of Hd. Qrs. Sections 1 & 2 and B.2 Echelon. Lieut F.M. STERRY joined the Column from 34th D.A.C. and was posted to the 282 nd Army field Artg. B.A.C.	
	26-1-17		The Column was inspected by Major-General C.P.A. HULL. C.B. Cmdg. XI Corps. The animals of the Column were inspected by the C.R.A. 56. Division and the D.D.V.S. first Army.	

9. G. Griffith Lt. Col. R.F.A.
Comdg. 56. D.A.C.

SECRET

WAR DIARY

56ᵀᴴ DIV. AMMN. COL.

FEBRUARY – 1917.

Army Form C. 2118

WAR DIARY
or
INTELLIGENCE SUMMARY
(Erase heading not required.)

56th DIVISIONAL AMMUNITION COLUMN R.F.A
FEBRUARY 1917

Place	Date	Hour	Summary of Events and Information	Remarks and references to Appendices
As shown	12/2/17		Positions of the sections of the 56th D.A.C on 1-2-17	
			Headquarters L.26.b.1.2	
			No 1 Section R.11. Central	Map Reference:-
			No 2 Section L.26. d.2.8	FRANCE Sheet 36A.
			No 3 Section L.36. a. & 2	
			Lieut. R.T.E. MASSEY to Hospital	
	14/2/17		Lieut. H.C. BROOKES to Hospital	
	19/2/17		Lieut. F.E. WEBB. R.F.A (S.R) Posted to 56 D.A.C	
			Lieut. F.E. BROOKES from Hospital	
			Lieut. W.H. DEASON having been evacuated to England, sick, is struck off	
			Strength Arty:- G.H.Q. Lay No 677 of 17-2-17	
	19/2/17		Lieut. F.J. WELDON-TAYLOR to Hospital	
	20/2/17		Major G.C. COTTON DEN. YEO. Posted to 56 Divn & taken on the strength of 56 DAC	
	26/2/17		Lieut. R.T.E. MASSEY from Hospital	

J.J. Cotton Major For Lieut Col R.F.A.
Commanding 56th Divl. Ammn Col

Vol 18

SECRET.

War Diary

56. D.A.C.

March 1914

Army Form C. 2118

WAR DIARY
or
INTELLIGENCE SUMMARY

(Erase heading not required.)

56 DIVISIONAL AMMUNITION COLUMN.

MARCH 1914.

Place	Date	Hour	Summary of Events and Information	Remarks and references to Appendices
	1-3-17		Positions of the Sections of the 56 D.A.C. on 1-3-17:-	
			Head Quarters L 26 b.12.) Map Reference.	
			Section No 1. R 11. Central.)	
			" No 2. L 26. D.2.8.) FRANCE Sheet 36A.	
			" No 3. L 36 A.8.2.)	
CALONNE	5.3.17		The D.A.C. left the above positions and marched to CALONNE.	
WITTERNESSE	7.3.17 8.3.17		" " " " " " " WITTERNESSE.	
BERGUENEUSE	9.3.17		" " " " " " " BERGUENEUSE.	
BOUBERS	10.3.17		" " " " " " " BOUBERS sur CANCHE.	
GROUCHES	13.3.17		" " " " " " " GROUCHES.	
			Head Quarters Sections 1 & 3 left GROUCHES and marched to LUCHEUX.	
			Section No 2 left GROUCHES and marched to SIMENCOURT.	
LUCHEUX	14.3.17		Head Quarters, Section 1 & 3 left LUCHEUX marched to BAVINCOURT.	
BAVINCOURT	19.3.17		" BAVINCOURT and marched to SIMENCOURT.	
SIMENCOURT	—		Head Quarters & Sections 1,2, & 3, in Camp at Q 16 Central, Map Reference 51o.	
			Supplying ammunition nightly.	
BAVINCOURT	18.3.17		Lieut F.J. WELDON TAYLOR rejoined from Hospital.	
"	18.3.17		Capt. M.J. SMITH O.C. Sec. 1. admitted to 4 Field Ambulance.	
"	18.3.17		MAJOR C.E. COTTON assumed Command of No 1 Section.	

Q.W. E. Wyf.
Lt. Col. R.F.A.
Comdg. 56 D.A.C.

Army Form C. 2118

WAR DIARY
or
INTELLIGENCE SUMMARY

56 DIVISIONAL AMMUNITION COLUMN

MARCH 1919.

(Erase heading not required.)

Instructions regarding War Diaries and Intelligence Summaries are contained in F.S. Regs., Part II. and the Staff Manual respectively. Title Pages will be prepared in manuscript.

Place	Date	Hour	Summary of Events and Information	Remarks and references to Appendices
			Extract from Part II orders of 24-3-19.	
			Lt.Col. GRIFFITH. E.W. Head Quarters 56.D.A.C. Mentioned in Despatches. (Auth. Supplement to London Gazette Jany 4th 1917)	
			Lieut STORRAR. J.S. Head Quarters 56.D.A.C. Mentioned in Despatches (Auth. Supplement to London Gazette Jany. 4th 1917)	

R.W.Forfar
Lt. Col. R.F.A.
Comdg. 56 D.A.C.

Vol 19.

56 Div. Ammn Col R.F.A

War Diary.

April 1917

R

Army Form C. 2118

WAR DIARY
or
INTELLIGENCE SUMMARY

56 DIVISIONAL AMMUNITION COLUMN

APRIL 1917.

(Erase heading not required.)

Instructions regarding War Diaries and Intelligence Summaries are contained in F.S. Regs., Part II. and the Staff Manual respectively. Title Pages will be prepared in manuscript.

Place	Date	Hour	Summary of Events and Information	Remarks and references to Appendices
SIMENCOURT	1/4/17		The whole Column in Rutments at SIMENCOURT. Capt M.J. SMITH evacuated to England sick. Delivery of ammunition carried out by means of packs. Lieut C.H. WOOLRYCH and 2Lt R.A. WEISS joined the Column.	
SIMENCOURT & AGNY	13-4-17		The Column moved from SIMENCOURT to AGNY.	
AGNY	15-4-17		2Lt G.S. BRIDGES to Fd Amb. sick.	
AGNY	26-4-17		Capt A.H. MOREING left for England to take up an appointment here. 2Lieut G.S. BRIDGES evacuated to England sick.	
AGNY	29-4-17		Lieut C.H. WOOLRYCH joined 109 Battery 281 Bde R.F.A. 2Lieut G.L. PRIESTLY joined the Column.	

[signature]
Lt Col R.F.A.
Comdg 56 DAC

Vol 20

War Diary

56 D.A.C.

May. 1917

Army Form C. 2118

WAR DIARY
or
INTELLIGENCE SUMMARY

(Erase heading not required.)

56 DIVISIONAL AMMUNITION COLUMN.

MAY 1917.

Place	Date	Hour	Summary of Events and Information	Remarks and references to Appendices
A.C.N.Y.	2·5·17		The Column at A.C.N.Y. M.R. D.3. Sheet 51B.	
A.C.N.Y.	14·5·17		2Lt. G.L. Priestly to 281 Bde. R.H.A. for duty.	
A.C.N.Y.	19·5·17		2Lt. S.F. WEBB attached to 281 Bde. R.F.A. for instruction.	
A.C.N.Y.	20·5·17		2Lt. E.B. GREENWALL & 2Lt. W.L. EVANS joined the Column from England.	
A.C.N.Y.	23·5·17		Lieut F.J. WELDON TAYLOR to Third Army Artillery school for instruction.	
			The Column moved from A.C.N.Y:-	
			A Echelon and Head Quarters to S.10.D.88. } Map Ref Sheet. 51B.	
S.10.D.88	30·5·17		B Echelon - - - - to S.2.D.59. } Map Ref Sheet No. 2.	
" "	31·5·17		Major A.C. PATON joined the Column.	
			Major A.C. PATON assumed Command of Echelon No. 2.	
			Extract from Part II Orders	
			Extract from London Gazette 15·5·17.	
			Mentioned in Dispatches for devotion to duty & services in the field:-	
			Lieut (Temp Captain) A.H. MOREING.	
			P.A. HARRISON.	
			T. ALSTON. Battery Sergeant Major.	
			No. 34656	

Q B Tuthill
Lt Col. R.F.A.
Comdg. 56. D.A.C.

Vol 21

War Diary

June 1917

56 D.A.C.

Army Form C. 2118

WAR DIARY
or
INTELLIGENCE SUMMARY
(Erase heading not required.)

56 DIVISIONAL AMMUNITION COLUMN

JUNE 1917

Instructions regarding War Diaries and Intelligence Summaries are contained in F. S. Regs., Part II. and the Staff Manual respectively. Title Pages will be prepared in manuscript.

Place	Date	Hour	Summary of Events and Information	Remarks and references to Appendices
S.10.d.88.	3-6-17		A Echelon moved from S.10.d.88. to S.8.A.51. {Map Ref. Sheet 51 B} A Echelon at S.10.d.88. D Echelon at S.2.d.59	
S.8.A.51	27-6-17		2 Lt. C.J. EDWARDS joined the Column. Extract from London Gazette d/15-6-14. 2 Lt. (temp Lieut) J.S. Storrar R.F.A. awarded the Military Cross for devotion to duty, and services rendered in the field.	

E.W. [?] Lt. Col. R.F.A.
Comdg. 56. D.A.C.

1875 Wt. W593/826 1,000,000 4/15 J.B.C. & A. A.D.S.S./Forms/C. 2118.

Vol 22

War Diary.
56 D.A.C. R.H.A.

July 1917.

Army Form C. 2118.

WAR DIARY
or
INTELLIGENCE SUMMARY.

(Erase heading not required.)

56 DIVISIONAL AMMUNITION COLUMN.

July 1914.

Instructions regarding War Diaries and Intelligence Summaries are contained in F. S. Regs., Part II. and the Staff Manual respectively. Title pages will be prepared in manuscript.

Place	Date	Hour	Summary of Events and Information	Remarks and references to Appendices
S.8.A.51.	1-7-17		"A" Echelon at S.8.A.51. } Map ref Sheet 51B.	
	2-7-17		"B" Echelon at S.2.D.5.9. } Map ref Sheet 51B.	
			2Lt. C.J. EDWARDS posted to 280 Bde. R.F.A.	
COULLEMONT	5-7-17		The Column moved to COULLEMONT.	
CANETTEMONT	6-7-17		The Column moved from COULLEMONT to CANETTEMONT.	
CROIX	7-7-17		" " " " CANETTEMONT to CROIX.	
	9-7-17		" " " " CROIX to NEDONCHELLE.	
NEDONCHELLE	10-7-17		" " " " NEDONCHELLE to NEUFPRE.	
NEUFPRE	11-7-17		" " " " NEUFPRE to D'OXELAERE.	
D'OXELAERE	12-7-17		" " " " D'OXELAERE to EECKE.	
EECKE	13-7-17		" " " " EECKE to OUDEZEELE.	
OUDEZEELE	15-7-17		Lt. R.A. WEISS posted to 56 French Mortar Battery.	
OUDEZEELE	29-7-17		moved from OUDEZEELE to STEENWOORDE (K15.c.B.1. Sheet 27 1/40,000 Belgium & France)	
STEENWOORDE	30-7-17		moved from STEENWOORDE to H.26.b.7.5 Map Ref Sheet 24 1/40,000 Belgium & France.	

31/7/17

[signature]
Major
for Lt.Col.R.F.A.
Comdg. 56 D.A.C.

Vol 23

War Diary

56 D.A.C.

R.F.A

August 1914

Army Form C. 2118.

WAR DIARY
or
INTELLIGENCE SUMMARY.
(Erase heading not required.)

50 DIVISIONAL AMMUNITION COLUMN
August. 1914

Place	Date	Hour	Summary of Events and Information	Remarks and references to Appendices
				1/40,000 Belgium & France Sheet 28
H 26. b.7.5.	1-8-14		The Column at H 26.b.4.5. Sheet 28	
	4-8-14		B. Echelon with one subsection of Section No 1 moved H 29 c. 2.8. This portion of the Column acted as a forward pack section consisting of 300 animals, and carried ammunition up to the gun positions, by means of pack carriers.	
H 26. b.4.5	22.8.14		2 Lt E.B. GREENWALL. R.F.A. having been GASSED on 20th inst, when delivering ammunition, proceeded to 4 Field Ambulance on 22-8-14.	
H 26. b.4.5	24.8.14		Lieut R.T.E. MASSEY R.F.A. proceeded to the BASE for Medical Reclassification. The following is an extract from II Corps R.O. No 982 d. 26-8-14. Under authority delegated by the Field-Marshal Commanding in Chief, the Corps Commander has awarded the Military Medal to the undermentioned N.C.O. and men for gallantry and devotion to duty in action:- No 94154 Sergt J.W.WALLWARK (56 DAC.) No 103834 Dr A. MARTIN (56 DAC.) " 49426 Gnr J. RYLES " " 949690 Dr C. LANG " " 944485 Dr G. TURNER. " " 91235 Dr A. SMITH " (BAR TO)	
	31/8/17			R Wyatt Lieut Col. R.F.A. Comdg 50 D.A.C.

(A7092) Wt. W12859/M1293- 750,000. 1/17. D. D. & L., Ltd. Forms/C.2118/14.

Vol 24

War Diary.

5½ D.A.C.

September 1917.

Army Form C. 2118.

WAR DIARY
or
INTELLIGENCE SUMMARY.
(Erase heading not required.)

56 DIVISIONAL AMMUNITION COLUMN.

September 1914.

Place	Date	Hour	Summary of Events and Information	Remarks and references to Appendices
H.26.D.4.5.	2-9-17		Head Quarters and sections 1 & 2 at H.26 D. 4.5. B.Echelon at H.29 C.28. Sheet 28 1/40,000 Belgium & France	
OXELAERE	3-9-17		Column moved to OXELAERE.	
BAPAUME	4-9-17		Column entrained (CASSEL Station) for BAPAUME.	
N.4.d.6.8.	11-9-17		Column detrained (BAPAUME Station) proceeded to N.4.d. 6.8. Sheet 57c 1/40,000 France.	
"	14-9-17		Lieut. D.C.N. COOK posted to the Column.	
"	15-9-17		A.Echelon moved from N.4.d.6.8. to H.35 Central (Sheet 57c)	
H.35.c.Central	15-9-17		B.Echelon moved from N.4.d.6.8. to J.24.c Central (Sheet 57c)	
			B.Echelon re-organized to conform to new War Establishment Part VIIa. (No 642) d 4-8-17. Ceased to be known as B.Echelon. Designated in future S.A.A. Section.	
H.35.c Central	17-9-17		The following supplies to Establishment consequent on re-organisation disposed of as under:-	
			To 280 Bde R.F.A. 2 Sergts, 1 Saddler, 1Cpl S.S. 12 Drivers, 10 Gunners, & 26 Animals.	
			To 281 " 1 Cpl, 1 Bdr, 12 Drivers and 18 animals.	
			To H.T. Depot ABBEVILLE 19 Drivers 38 animals, 18 G.S. wagons, one Maltese Cart.	
			HONOURS AND REWARDS.	
			Under authority granted by His Majesty the King, the Field Marshall Commanding-in-Chief has awarded the following decorations to the undermentioned Officers and N.C.O.s & men:-	
			to 2 Lt. (A/Capt.) J.S. STORRAR, M.C. R.A. BAR to the MILITARY CROSS.	
			56 D.A.C. R.F.A.	
			to Lieut H.C. BROOKS. MILITARY CROSS.	
			56 D.A.C. R.F.A.	
			to No 91409 B.Q.M.S. MASON. H.G. MILITARY MEDAL.	
			" 681911 Sergt ASHURST. R. } No 1 Section 56 D.A.C. R.F.A. (D.R.O. No 1940 d 21-9-17)	
			" 60285 Driver GARDNER. H. }	

R.L. [signature] Lt.Col R.F.A.
Comdg 56 D.A.C.

Vol 25

War Diary

October 1914.

56 D.A.C. R.F.A.

Army Form C. 2118.

WAR DIARY
or
INTELLIGENCE SUMMARY.

56 DIVISIONAL AMMUNITION COLUMN.

OCTOBER. 1914

Place	Date	Hour	Summary of Events and Information	Remarks and references to Appendices
H 35 Central	6:10:17		Hd Qrs. & Sections 1 & 2 at H.35 Central } Sheet 54c. 1/40,000 S.A.A. Section at J.24.c Central	
—	12:10:17		Lieut Genl Sir C.L. WOOLLCOMBE K.C.B. G.O.C. IV Corps inspected the Column. Lieut & J. WELDON TAYLOR attached to Q Anti Aircraft Battery to undergo one month's course of instruction.	
—	24:10:17		Lieut. W.B. TURNER proceeded to the base for medical reclassification.	
—	27:10:17		Lieut W. BENYON W. Northamptonshire Regt. joined the Column.	

E.W. Ruffk
Lt. Col. R.F.A.
Commanding 56 D.A.C. R.F.A.

Vol 26

War Diary
56 D.A.C.

NOVEMBER 1917

Army Form C. 2118.

WAR DIARY
or
INTELLIGENCE SUMMARY.

56 DIVISIONAL AMMUNITION COLUMN R.F.A.

NOVEMBER 1917.

(Erase heading not required.)

Place	Date	Hour	Summary of Events and Information	Remarks and references to Appendices
H.35.c.Central	1-11-17		Head Quarters and Sections 1 & 2 at H.35 Central. Sheet 54c. 1/40.000. S.A.A. Section at J.24.c Central	
"	2-11-17		Lieut. D.C.N. COOK transferred to Royal Flying Corps.	
"	10-11-17		Lieut. F.J. WELDON TAYLOR rejoined from attachment to Anti Aircraft Battery	
"	25-11-17		Lieut. W.B. TURNER classified Permanent Base and struck off strength 25-11-17.	

30/11/17

R. Griffith
Lt. Col. R.F.A.
Comdg. 56. D.A.C. R.F.A.

Vol 27

War Diary

December 1917.

56 D.A.C. R.F.A.

Army Form C. 2118

WAR DIARY
or
INTELLIGENCE SUMMARY
(Erase heading not required.)

56 DIVISIONAL AMMUNITION COLUMN. R.F.A.

DECEMBER 1917.

Instructions regarding War Diaries and Intelligence Summaries are contained in F.S. Regs., Part II. and the Staff Manual respectively. Title Pages will be prepared in manuscript.

Place	Date	Hour	Summary of Events and Information	Remarks and references to Appendices
	1-12-17		Head Quarters & Sections 1 & 2 at H 35 Central.} Sheet 51c. 1/40,000 S.A.A. Section at J. 24.c. Central	
H 35 Central	14-12-17		The Column moved from H 35 Central & J 24.c. Central to COURCELLE-LE-CONTE.	
COURCELLE -LE-CONTE.	15-12-17		The Column moved from COURCELLE-LE-CONTE to GOUVES.	
GOUVES	16-12-17		The Column moved from GOUVES to ANZIN.	
			Extract from London Gazette dated 14th December 1914. Mentioned in despatches.	
			Lt. Col. E.W. GRIFFITH. R.F.A.	
			Capt. W.S. WATSON. R.F.A.	
			Extract from Corps Routine Orders.	
			Under Authority delegated by Field Marshal Commanding-in-chief, the G.O.C. VI Corps, has awarded the Military Medal to the under-mentioned N.C.O.:-	
			No. 85480 Sgt MOGG. E. No 1 Section 56. D.A.C.	

A.C. [signature]
Major for Lt.Col. R.F.A.
Comdg 56 D.A.C.

[Stamp: DIVISIONAL AMMUNITION COLUMN 31 DEC. 1917]

Vol 28

War Diary.

Jany 1918.

56 D.A.C. R.F.A.

Army Form C. 2118

WAR DIARY
or
INTELLIGENCE SUMMARY

56 DIVISIONAL AMMUNITION COLUMN. R.F.A.

JANUARY 1918.

(Erase heading not required.)

Instructions regarding War Diaries and Intelligence Summaries are contained in F.S. Regs., Part II. and the Staff Manual respectively. Title Pages will be prepared in manuscript.

Place	Date	Hour	Summary of Events and Information	Remarks and references to Appendices
ANZIN.	1-1-18		Head Quarters and 3 Sections at ANZIN.	
ANZIN.	1-1-18		Lt. Col. Griffith. E.W. D.S.O. R.F.A. Struck off strength. (Medical Board Ordered. War Office A.G.40.)	
ANZIN.	15-1-18		The Column moved from ANZIN to GAUCHIN-LEGAL.	
GAUCHIN-LEGAL.	21-1-18		MAJOR. J.W. CARDEN. T.D., R.F.A., joined the Column and assumed Command. 1-1-18.	
			Extract from London Gazette (Supplement) of	
			Awarded. D.S.O.	
			T/Lieut. Colonel. E.W. GRIFFITH. R.F.A.	
	31-1-18			

James W Carden Major R.F.A.
Comdg. 56.D.A.C.R.F.A.

Stamp: DIVISIONAL AMMUNITION COLUMN W563. 31 JAN 1918.

Army Form C. 2118.

'WAR' DIARY
or
INTELLIGENCE SUMMARY.
(Erase heading not required.)

FEBRUARY 1918.

56 DIVISIONAL AMMUNITION COLUMN.

WM 29

Place	Date	Hour	Summary of Events and Information	Remarks and references to Appendices
GAUCHIN-LEGAL	1-2-18		Lieut F.J. WELDON-TAYLOR R.F.A. struck off strength. Authority A.G./3226 (O) 1-2-18.	
GAUCHIN-LEGAL	1-2-18		Hd. Qrs. & 3 Sections at GAUCHIN-LEGAL. (P 80 Central Sheet 36B).	
GAUCHIN-LEGAL	4-2-18		Major A.C. PATON. Comdg Section No. 2 granted 3 months leave commencing 1-2-18. Authority A.G. 441/528/P.S. d/31-1-18.	
GAUCHIN-LEGAL	8-2-18		Major G.E.F. COTTON (Denbigh Yeomanry) struck off strength with effect from 23-1-18. Authority A.G. 3369 (O) d/9-2-18	
GAUCHIN-LEGAL	16-2-18		The Column moved from GAUCHIN-LEGAL to ANZIN. (G.S. Central Sheet 51B).	
ANZIN	27-2-18		Major General F.A. DUDGEON C.B. G.O.C. 56 Division, inspected the Column.	
ANZIN	28-2-18		The undermentioned Officers were attached to the D.A.C. on the dates shown:—	
			on 13-2-18. 2Lt. J.E. CLOSE. from 281 Bde. R.F.A.	
			" 18-2-18 2Lt. W.J. LAWN. from 281 Bde. R.F.A.	
			" 18-2-18 2Lt. A. WORTH. from 280 Bde. R.F.A.	
			" 28-2-18 2Lt. H.B. PRITCHARD from 280 Bde. R.F.A.	
	28-2-18			

Francis M. Gordon Major R.F.A.
Comdg. 56. D.A.C. R.F.A.

War Diary.
56 D.A.C.
February 1918

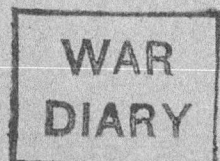

56th DIVISIONAL AMMUNITION COLUMN, R.F.A.

M A R C H

1 9 1 8

War Diary.
56 D.A.C. R.F.A.

March 1918

Army Form C. 2118

WAR DIARY
or
INTELLIGENCE SUMMARY

56 DIVISIONAL AMMUNITION COLUMN.

MARCH 1918.

(Erase heading not required.)

Place	Date	Hour	Summary of Events and Information	Remarks and references to Appendices
ANZIN.	24-3-18		Extract from London Gazette, Supplement March 28th. R.H. & R.Y.A. MAJOR J.W. GARDEN to Lieut. Colonel. (Jany 28. 1918)	
	30-3-18.			Camilla Garden Lieut Colonel. R.Y.A. Comdg 56 D.A.C. R.Y.A.

1873 Wt. W593/826 1,000,000 4/15 J.B.C. & A. A.D.S.S./Forms/C. 2118.

WAR DIARY
or
INTELLIGENCE SUMMARY

(Erase heading not required.)

56 DIVISIONAL AMMUNITION COLUMN.

MARCH 1918.

Army Form C. 2118.

Instructions regarding War Diaries and Intelligence Summaries are contained in F.S. Regs., Part II. and the Staff Manual respectively. Title Pages will be prepared in manuscript.

Place	Date	Hour	Summary of Events and Information	Remarks and references to Appendices
ANZIN.	1-3-18		Hd. Qrs. and 3 Sections at ANZIN. (G & Bental. Sheet 51 B.)	
ANZIN	4-3-18		2Lt J.E. CLOSE attached from 281 Bde R.F.A. taken on the strength of the Column with effect from 1-3-18.	
ANZIN	5-3-18		MAJOR A.E. PATON struck off strength with effect from 6-2-18. Authy A.G. 441/529/P.S.A/31-1-18.	
ANZIN	5-3-18		2Lt A. WORTH. ceased to be attached to the Column, and rejoined 280 Bde R.F.A.	
ANZIN	5-3-18		2Lt A.A. PURVIS attached to the Column from 280 Bde R.F.A.	
ANZIN	20-3-18		Lieut J.R.G. JORGENSON appointed Staff Captain to 15th Divisional Artillery and struck off strength of the Column.	
ANZIN	20-3-18		Capt J.S. STORRAR. ceased to perform the duties of Adjutant, and assumed Command of Section No. 1.	
ANZIN	21-3-18		Lieut R.A. HARRISON. appointed ADJUTANT. and allowed to wear the badges of the rank of Captain, pending appearance in Gazette. (Authy (g) O.C retained)	
ANZIN	21-3-18		Lieut W.W. BENYON. assumed Command of Section No 2. and allowed to wear the badges of the rank of Captain pending notification in Gazette. (Authy (g) O.C retained)	
ANZIN	21-3-18		Lieut W.H. CARTER proceeded to England, on posting to Reserve Battalion Welsh Guards, struck off strength. (Authy N°2 Bnthy Yeo. 303 (M.S.1.T.)	
ANZIN	28-3-18		2Lt H.W. THIRTLE joined the Column.	

James A Gordon Lt. Col. R.F.A.
Cmmd 56 D.A.C.

56th Divisional Artillery.

56th DIVISIONAL AMMUNITION COLUMN R.F.A.

APRIL 1918.

Army Form C. 2118.

WAR DIARY
or
INTELLIGENCE SUMMARY.
(Erase heading not required.)

56 DIVISIONAL AMMUNITION COLUMN.

APRIL. 1918.

Instructions regarding War Diaries and Intelligence Summaries are contained in F. S. Regs., Part II. and the Staff Manual respectively. Title pages will be prepared in manuscript.

Place	Date	Hour	Summary of Events and Information	Remarks and references to Appendices
ANZIN.	2-4-18		Hd.Q rs and 3 Sections at ANZIN.	
F.22d 6.0.	8-4-18		The Column moved from ANZIN to F 22 D.6.0. sheet 51c	
MONTENESCOURT	14-4-18		The Column moved from F22 d 6.0. to MONTENESCOURT.	
SIMENCOURT			The Column moved from MONTENESCOURT to SIMENCOURT	
			2/Lt A. FIRMIN. 2Lt. J. W. KELLY and 2Lt. W.O.S. WALLACE joined the Column.	
"	20-4-18		2/Lt THIRTLE. H.W. proceeded to T.M. Batteries for duty.	
"	22-4-18		2Lt. PRITCHARD. H.B. rejoined 280 Bde R.F.A. for duty.	
"	24-4-18		Capt. J. McA. SCOTT. R.A.M.C. Proceeded to 2/2 London Fd. Amb. for duty.	
"	24-4-18		Capt. M.A. OULTON. C.A.M.C. joined the Column and took over the duties of M.O. I/c.	
	30-4-18			

James McGarder
Lt. Col. R.F.A.
Comdg 56 D.A.C.

Vol 32

W 382

War Diary.

56 D.A.C. R.F.A.

May. 1918.

Army Form C. 2118.

WAR DIARY
or
INTELLIGENCE SUMMARY.

56 DIVISIONAL AMMUNITION COLUMN. R.F.A.

MAY, 1918.

(Erase heading not required.)

Instructions regarding War Diaries and Intelligence Summaries are contained in F. S. Regs., Part II. and the Staff Manual respectively. Title pages will be prepared in manuscript.

Place	Date	Hour	Summary of Events and Information	Remarks and references to Appendices
SIMENCOURT	1-5-18		Hd. Qrs. and 3 Sections at SIMENCOURT.	
"	5-5-18		Hd. Qrs. and Sections 1&2. moved to MONTENESCOURT.	
MONTENES-COURT	19-5-18		S.A.A. Section moved from SIMENCOURT to MONTENESCOURT.	
"	24-5-18		The Indian Personnel joined the Column.	
			Extract from London Gazette Supplement of 21-5-18.	
			Mentioned in despatches.	
			Lieut. Col. J.W. GARDEN. T.D. R.F.A.	
			80514 B.S.M. ANDREWS. J.	
	31-5-18			

James W Garden Lt. Col. R.F.A.
Comdg. 56 D.A.C.

"SECRET"

WAR DIARY

56th Div. Ammn. Column

JUNE, 1918

Army Form C. 2118.

WAR DIARY
or
INTELLIGENCE SUMMARY. 56TH DIVL. AMMN. COLUMN. R.F.A.

JUNE 1918.

(Erase heading not required.)

Instructions regarding War Diaries and Intelligence Summaries are contained in F. S. Regs., Part II. and the Staff Manual respectively. Title pages will be prepared in manuscript.

Place	Date	Hour	Summary of Events and Information	Remarks and references to Appendices
MONTENESCOURT	9/6/18		Headquarters and three sections at MONTENESCOURT.	
"	22/6/18		Lieut. A.H. THOMAS to R.H. & R.F.A. Base Depot for medical re-classification. Lieut. A.H. THOMAS rejoins unit from First Army Artillery School and Reinforcement Camp.	
			HONOURS and REWARDS.	
			Extract from Supplement to London Gazette dated JUNE 2nd, 1918	
			D. S. O.	
			Lt. Colonel. J.W. GARDEN, R.F.A.	
			Under authority delegated by His Majesty the King, the G.O.C. XVIIth Corps has awarded the MILITARY MEDAL to the u/m.	
			No. 98587 Corpl. BUCKINGHAM, H. No. 1 Section	
			Authority:- XVIIth Corps No. A. 6/495 dt: 14-5-18.	

30/6/18

James Garden
Lieut. Colonel R.F.A.
Comdg. 56th D.A.C.

(A7092). Wt. W12839/M1293. 750,000. 1/17. D. D. & L., Ltd. Forms/C.2118/14.

WR 34

War Diary.
56 D.A.C.

July 1918.

Army Form C. 2118.

WAR DIARY
or
INTELLIGENCE SUMMARY. 56 DIVISIONAL AMMUNITION COLUMN.

(Erase heading not required.)   JULY. 1918.

Instructions regarding War Diaries and Intelligence Summaries are contained in F. S. Regs., Part II. and the Staff Manual respectively. Title pages will be prepared in manuscript.

Place	Date	Hour	Summary of Events and Information	Remarks and references to Appendices
MONTENESCOURT	1-7-18		Hd Qrs and three sections at MONTENESCOURT.	
	6-7-18		Consequent on reorganization of Amm. Wagons from six to four mule teams, 22 Drivers were sent to 1st Army Re-inforcement Camp, and 50 Mules to No. 4 Base Remount Depot Boulogne. Authy. G.H.Q. Letter O.B./1866/E d/ 10-6-18.	
"	17-7-18		2 Lt J.M.RIMMER.R.F.A. joined the Column.	
"	22-7-18		The Column moved from MONTENESCOURT to GAUCHIN - LEGAL.	

31-7-18.

James A Goodie
Lt. Col. R.F.A.
Comdg. 56 D.A.C.

31 JULY 1918

WR 35

War Diary

57 D.A.C.

August 1918

W850
31 AUG. 1918

Army Form C. 2118.

WAR DIARY
or
INTELLIGENCE SUMMARY.

56 DIVISIONAL AMMUNITION COLUMN.

AUGUST. 1918.

(Erase heading not required.)

Instructions regarding War Diaries and Intelligence Summaries are contained in F. S. Regs., Part II. and the Staff Manual respectively. Title pages will be prepared in manuscript.

Place	Date	Hour	Summary of Events and Information	Remarks and references to Appendices
GAUCHIN-LEGAL.	1-8-18		The Column moved from GAUCHIN-LEGAL to MONTENESCOURT.	
MONTENESCOURT	22-8-18		S.A.A. Section moved to BEAUMETZ. Detached from the Column to operate with the Infantry.	
—	23-8-18		Hd Qrs and Sections 1&2 moved from MONTENESCOURT to LE-FERMONT.	
LE FERMONT	24-8-18		S.A.A. Section moved from BEAUMETZ to BRETENCOURT.	
"	26-8-18		S.A.A. Section moved from BRETENCOURT to 3.15.b.2.4. (Sheet 51B).	
"	29-8-18		H.Q. & Sections 1&2 moved to 3.11.0.44. (Sheet 51B.)	

Monro Capt. RFA
for Lt. Col. Comdg. 56 D.A.C.

Vol 36

War Diary,
September 1918

56 D.A.C.

Army Form C. 2118

WAR DIARY
or
INTELLIGENCE SUMMARY

(Erase heading not required.)

56 DIVISIONAL AMMUNITION COLUMN.   SEPTEMBER. 1918.

Instructions regarding War Diaries and Intelligence Summaries are contained in F.S. Regs., Part II. and the Staff Manual respectively. Title Pages will be prepared in manuscript.

Place	Date	Hour	Summary of Events and Information	Remarks and references to Appendices
S 11.C.4.4.	1-9-18		Hd. Qrs. & Sections 1 & 2 at S 11 C 4.4. S Sect 51 B. S.A.A. Section at S.15 v 2.4.	
	3-9-18		Section 1 moved to T 2 D Central. Section 2 to T 28 v 9.8.	
T 2 D Cent.	4-9-18		Hd. Qrs. moved to T 2 D Central.	
—	5-9-18		Hd. Qrs. and Section 1 moved to T 28 v 9.8.	
T 28 v 9.8.	6-9-18		Hd. Qrs. Sections 1 & 2 moved to T 2 D Central.	
T 2 D Cent.	7-9-18		Hd. Qrs. Sections 1 & 2 moved to N 15 A Central. S.A.A. Section moved to N 24 c.5.2.	
N 15 A. Cent.	9-9-18		Lieut J.W. SMITH (General List) joined the Column – for Indian Personnel.	
"	12-9-18		Lieut Col. H.J. CURLEY. T.D. R.F.A. joined the Column.	
"	14-9-18		2 Lt T.C. LEWORTHY. R.F.A. joined the Column.	
"	14-9-18		Capt M.A. OULTON. C.A.M.C. Medical Officer i/c unit, left for duty at First Canadian Stationary Hospital.	
"	30-9-18		Hd. Qrs. Sections 1 & 2 moved to O 28 C Central. S.A.A. Section moved to Sheet 51 B.	

All map references are Sheet 51 B.

James W. Garden
Lt. Col. R.F.A.
Comdg 56 D.A.C. R.F.A.

War Diary.

56 D.A.C. R.F.A.

October 1918

WAR DIARY or INTELLIGENCE SUMMARY

Army Form C. 2118

OCTOBER 1918.

56 DIVISIONAL AMMUNITION COLUMN.

Place	Date	Hour	Summary of Events and Information	Remarks and references to Appendices
	1-10-18		Hd.Qrs. Sections 1 & 2 at O28 c. Central, S.A.A. Section at V.15 b. (Sheet 51 B).	
O28 c.Central	3-10-18		Lieut Col CURLEY. H.J. posted to Provisional Brigade Martin Eglise near Dieppe.	
"	8-10-18		H.Q. Sections 1 & 2 moved to V.14 Central.	
V.14 Central	8-10-18		Lieut A.H. THOMAS struck off strength. (Medically boarded in England).	
"	11-10-18		Capt J.E.T. JONES. R.A.M.C. took over the duties of M.O. to unit.	
"	16-10-18		S.A.A. Section moved from V.15 b to ANZIN.	
"	18-10-18		Hd.Qrs. Sections 1 & 2 moved to RUMAUCOURT. (Sheet 51 B).	
RUMAUCOURT	20-10-18		Hd.Qrs. Sections 1 & 2 " " MORENCHIES area. (Sheet 51 A).	
MORENCHIES	26-10-18		Hd.Qrs. Sections 1 & 2 " " IWUY.	
IWUY	30-10-18		Hd.Qrs. Sections 1 & 2 " " THIANT area. (HQ. at HAULCHIN. Sections 1 & 2 at MONCHAUX.	

Honours & Rewards

Under Authority delegated by His Majesty the King, the G.O.C. XXII Corps has awarded the M.M. to the undermentioned:-

4-10-18 No 2675 Sergt G.H. Darwick   No 2 Section.
"   No 947684 Corpl A/Sgt Large. A.G. No 1 Section.
12-10-18 " 80514 B.S.M. Andrews J.   No 7 Section.

Bar to M.M.

12-10-18 No 681911 Sergt Ashurst. R. M.M. No 7 Section.

31-10-18

James W Garden
Lt Col R.F.A.
Comdg 56 D.A.C.

Vol 38

War Diary

53 D.A.C.

November. 1918

Army Form C. 2118

WAR DIARY
or
INTELLIGENCE SUMMARY
(Erase heading not required.)

56 DIVISIONAL AMMUNITION COLUMN R.F.A.

NOVEMBER 1918.

Place	Date	Hour	Summary of Events and Information	Remarks and references to Appendices
HAULCHIN	1-11-18		H.Q. at HAULCHIN. Sections 1 & 2 at MONCHAUX. S.A.A. Section at ANZIN.	
"	1-11-18		S.A.A. Section moved to DOUCHY.	
"	2-11-18		Sections No 2 moved to HAULCHIN.	
"	4-11-18		Hd. Qrs. Sections 1, 2 & S.A.A. moved to AULNOY.	
AULNOY	6-11-18		Sections 1, 2 & S.A.A. moved to SAULTAIN.	
"	7-11-18		Hd. Qrs. moved to SAULTAIN.	
SAULTAIN	9-11-18		Hd. Qrs. Sections 1 & 2 moved to ONNEZIES, S.A.A. Section to FAYT-LE-FRANC.	
ONNEZIES	11-11-18		Armistice commenced at 1100 hours.	
"	26-11-18		S.A.A. Section moved from FAYT-LE-FRANC to HARVENG.	

Honours & Rewards.

Under authority delegated by the Government of India, the Field Marshal,
Commanding-in-Chief, has awarded the following decorations for Distinguished
Service in the Field:—

The Indian Distinguished Service Medal.

No. 33578 Dr. KISHAN. } No 2 Section.
No. 32515 Dr. CHOTTA.

Under authority delegated by His Majesty the King, the G.O.C. Canadian
Corps has awarded the Military Medal to the under mentioned:—

No. 947963 Sergt. E.A. SKILTON. S.A.A. Section.

James W. Gordon

Lt. Col. R.F.A.
Comdg. 56 D.A.C. R.F.A.

War Diary.
December 1918.
56 D.A.C. R.F.A.

Army Form C. 2118

WAR DIARY
or
INTELLIGENCE SUMMARY
(Erase heading not required.)

56 DIVISIONAL AMMUNITION COLUMN

DECEMBER 1918.

Instructions regarding War Diaries and Intelligence Summaries are contained in F. S. Regs., Part II. and the Staff Manual respectively. Title Pages will be prepared in manuscript.

Place	Date	Hour	Summary of Events and Information	Remarks and references to Appendices
ONNEZIES	1-12-18		H.Q. Sections 1 & 2 at ONNEZIES, SAA Section at HARVENG.	
CIPLY	6-12-18		H.Q. Sections 1 & 2 moved to CIPLY.	
	12-12-18		SAA Section moved to CIPLY.	
"	27-12-18		Lt. Col. J.W. GARDEN. D.S.O. T.D. R.F.A. granted leave to United Kingdom from 27-12-18 to 29-1-19. Authy. XXII Corps A 3368/96 /24-12-18. A.O.I. 2327. Honours & Awards. Extract from London Gazette. War Services. Sir Douglas Haig's list of mentions November 8th 1918. Lieut W.L. Evans. R.F.A. No 947555. Sergt. R.A. Robson.	
	31-12-18.			

W.S. Watson Capt. R.A.
for Lt Col. R.F.A.
Comdg. 56 D.A.C. R.F.A.

WAR DIARY *or* **INTELLIGENCE SUMMARY**

Army Form C. 2118

(Erase heading not required.) 56th DIVISIONAL AMMUNITION COLUMN

JANUARY 1919

Place	Date	Hour	Summary of Events and Information	Remarks and references to Appendices
CIPLY	1.1.19		H.Q. No I. No II. & S.A.A. Sections at HYON - CIPLY.	
"	12.1.19		2/Lieut J. M. RIMMER left for Dispersal Area & Struck off Strength	
"	20.1.19		Lieut W. L. EVANS left for Dispersal Area & Struck off Strength	
"	27.1.19		2/Lieut J. H. KELLY left for Dispersal Area	

J Moroy
Capt R.F.A.
for Lieut Col. R.F.A.
Commanding 56th D.A.C.

WAR DIARY
INTELLIGENCE SUMMARY

Army Form C. 2118

(Erase heading not required.)

56TH DIVISIONAL AMMN. COLUMN.

FEBRUARY, 1919

Place	Date	Hour	Summary of Events and Information	Remarks and references to Appendices
C.I.PLY.	1/2/19		Ad. Qrs., No.1 Section, No.2 Section & S.A.A. Section at HYON-C.I.PLY.	9841
—	29/1/19		Lt. Col. J.W. GARDEN, D.S.O. R.F.A. Having been demobilized while on leave to U.K. struck off Strength. Auth: W.O. (9.6.4.a) dt. 17/2/1919.	
—	—		Capt. W.S. WATSON, R.F.A., appointed to command 56-D.A.C. (with effect from 30/1/19) Vice Lt. Col. J.W. GARDEN.	
—	—		Capt. A.C.R. CROOM-JOHNSON, M.C. R.F.A., posted to D.A.C. and is appointed to command S.A.A. Section, 56. D.A.C. (with effect from 30/1/19) "VICE" Capt. W.S. WATSON.	
—	6/2/19		2/Lt. A.A. FIRMIN, R.F.A, to No. 3 Base Remount Depot for duty.	
—	13/2/19		W.O.S. WALLACE, R.F.A, to Genl. Genl. Base Depot to collect party of 25 Indians for D.A.C.	

W Watson Captain R.F.A.,
Comdg. 56. D.A.C.

Army Form C. 2118

50 DIVISIONAL AMMN. COLUMN.
R.F.A.

MARCH 1919

WAR DIARY
INTELLIGENCE SUMMARY
(Erase heading not required.)

Place	Date	Hour	Summary of Events and Information	Remarks and references to Appendices
	1/3/19			
CIPLY	12/3/19		H.Q. No. 1129 Sec Section at Hybon C.1947.	
-	18/3/19		2/Lt R.F. FIRMIN, R.F.A. Posted to 281 Batt. R.F.A.	
-	20/3/19		J.A. THORNTON, R.F.A. Posted from 281 Bde R.F.A. Lieut (A/Capt) J.S. STORRAR, M.C. R.F.A. posted to command 109 Battery, R.F.A.	
-	18/3/19		Capt. R.F. HARRISON, R.F.A. returned from leave.	

W.S. Watson Capt R.F.A.
Comdg 50 D.A.C

Army Form C. 2118

WAR DIARY
INTELLIGENCE SUMMARY
56 Divisional Ammunition Column R.F.A

(Erase heading not required.)

Place	Date	Hour	Summary of Events and Information	Remarks and references to Appendices
Hylon-C.Plt.	1/4/19		H.Q. No 1. Section) as Non-C.Plt. -2-) -3- Sea)	
	6/4/19		Lieut L.W. GEE) W.J. LAWN) Posted to 156th Div. arty. J.E. CLOSS) Army of the Rhine. 2/Lt A.A. PURVIS)	
"	16/4/19		2/Lt. J.L. HOLME. Rejoined from Renown Staging Camp, VALENCIENNES.	
	16/4/19		2/Lt W.O.S WALLACE; retained at Ind. Genl. Base Depot.) Struck off Strength.	
	27/4/19		2/Lt. J.L HOLME to wear badges of higher rank, pending notification in London Gazette. (Auth. 56 Div. A/Q.X. 97/1186 dd. 26-4-19)	
	29/4/19		Capt. A.C.R. CROOM-JOHNSON, M.C. Granted leave to U.K. from 29-4-19 to 12-5-19.	

W.T. Watson Capt. R.F.A.
Comdg 56 D.A.C.

Army Form C. 2118

WAR DIARY
or
INTELLIGENCE SUMMARY
(Erase heading not required.)

Instructions regarding War Diaries and Intelligence Summaries are contained in F.S. Regs., Part II. and the Staff Manual respectively. Title Pages will be prepared in manuscript.

56th DIVISIONAL AMMUNITION COLUMN, R.F.A.
MAY 1919

WO 44

Place	Date	Hour	Summary of Events and Information	Remarks and references to Appendices
MONS-CIPLY	1/5/19		Hd. Qrs., No. 1 & 2 Sections & Sea Section at MYON-CIPLY.	
"	11/5/19		Capt. P.A.HARRISON, R.F.A.(T.F) to U.K. for Dispersal. Lieut. T.C. LEWORTHY, R.F.A.(T.C) to U.K. for repatriation.	Correct
"	13/5/19		Capt. A.C.R. CROON-JOHNSON, M.C., R.F.A.(T.F) returned from leave.	
"	15/5/19		Lieut. H.C. BROOKS, M.C, R.F.A. to U.K. for Dispersal.	
"	19/5/19		Hd. Qrs., No.1 & 2 Sections & Sea Section moved to JEMAPPES.	
JEMAPPES	25/5/19		Capt. J.E.T. JONES, R.A.M.C. (T.C) having left for Duty with No. 6. C.C.S., ceased to be attached to the D.A.C.	
"	26/5/19		Cadre of No.2. Section (1 Off., 50 ORs, all vehicles & stores) & Cadre of Sea Section proceeded to BULFORD (via ANTWERP & NEWHAVEN) for dispersal.	
"	27/5/19		Cadre of No.1. Section (1 off., 50 ORs, vehicles) & stores of No.1. Section & Sea Section) with 1 off. & 32 ORs, of Sea Section, proceeded to BULFORD (via ANTWERP & NEWHAVEN) for dispersal.	
"	29/5/19		Cadre of Hd. Qrs. (1 off. 18 ORs, vehicles & stores) with remainder of Sea Section Cadre (3 ORs) proceeded to BULFORD (via ANTWERP & NEWHAVEN) for dispersal.	

W.P. Watson Capt. R.F.A.
Commanding 56th Divisional Ammunition Column.

www.ingramcontent.com/pod-product-compliance
Lightning Source LLC
Chambersburg PA
CBHW080925230426
43668CB00014B/2201